Profiles and Profiling: a practical introduction

by
Gloria Hitchcock

Longman

LONGMAN GROUP UK LIMITED
*Longman House, Burnt Mill, Harlow, Essex CM20 2JE, England
and Associated Companies throughout the World*

First published 1986
Third impression 1987

ISBN 0 582 355060

Set in 10/12 *pt Linotron Plantin*

*Produced by Longman Singapore Publishers Pte Ltd
Printed in Singapore*

Contents

Acknowledgements

I would like to thank Geoffrey Crump, Director of Education, Alan Garnham, Principal Adviser, and Martin Clarke, Senior Adviser Secondary Education, in my Local Education Authority in the County of Avon. Their generous support and encouragement has been greatly appreciated.

I am particularly grateful to those who read the original manuscript, and whose stringent and constructive comments enabled significant improvements to be made: Hazel Johns, Adviser for Pastoral and Social Education, County of Avon; Peter March, Principal Adviser (Careers Education and Guidance), County of Avon; Patrick Bird, Head of Hengrove School; Renee Daines, Department of Social Work, University of Bristol; and Jean Shirley, Further Education Unit, Department of Education and Science.

Many teachers have given freely of both their time and material. Without their help this book would not have been possible, and my thanks go to all of them. Names of their schools are given below.

I am also grateful to the close friends and colleagues who encouraged me to persevere in the early stages.

Finally I would like to record my very special thanks to my long-suffering family.

I am grateful to the following for permission to reproduce copyright material:

Bayswater Centre for the Bayswater Profile; City and Guilds of London Institute for Profiles; County of Avon for Avon Student Profile; Deeside High School for Clwyd 16+ Profile; Dean Magna School, Mitcheldean – part of the West Gloucestershire scheme – for Profile; Evesham High School for Profile; FEU for extracts from 'The Avon Profile Initiative' by Gloria Hitchock in *Profiles in Action*; Havering Educational Computer Centre and University of Edinburgh (JIIG-CAL) for Adviser's Print 1 and 2; Halton Schools Industry Committee for Halton Profile; Joint Board Certificate of Pre-vocational Education for Profile; Hayesfield School, Bath for Profile; Helston School, Cornwall for Profile; Humberside County Council for Profile; Longman for extracts from *Computer-aided profiling*, first published by FEU; Longman Resource Unit for a

Profile from *Recording Achievement at 16+* by Brian Goacher; Macmillan for p. 25 of *Teach Yourself to Diagnose Reading Problems* by Ted Ames; Manpower Services Commission for 'Can-do cards' and Profiles; Market Weighton School, York for Profile; Phil Neale for Profile; Norton Priory School for Achievement Certificate; Pen Park School for Profile; Portway School, Bristol for Profile; Pupils' Personal Records for an extract from the *Tutors' Handbook*; The Royal Society of Arts Examinations Board for the SLAPONS Profile from *Profiles* published by the FEU, and Practical Communication Profile; SCDC Publications for an extract from *Profile Reporting in Wales* (Committee for Wales) 1983; The Scottish Council for Research in Education for an extract from *SCRE Profile Assessment System Manual*; Derek Sowden, Hartcliffe School for Profile; The Village College, Comberton for Record of Achievement; Wiltshire County Council for Record of Personal Achievement.

For Jane

List of abbreviations

CBI	Confederation of British Industry
CCDU	Counselling and Career Development Unit
CGLI	City and Guilds of London Institute
CPVE	Certificate of Pre-vocational Education
CSE	Certificate of Secondary Education
DES	Department of Education and Science
FEU	Further Education Unit (DES)
GCE	General Certificate of Education
GCSE	General Certificate of Secondary Education
HMI	Her Majesty's Inspectors
ILEA	Inner London Education Authority
JIIG – CAL	Job Ideas and Information Generator – Computer Assisted Learning
LAMSAC	Local Authority Management Services and Computer Committee
LEA	Local Education Authority
MSC	Manpower Services Commission
NRA	Northern Record of Achievement
OCEA	Oxford Certificate of Educational Achievement
PAR	Personal Achievement Record
PPR	Pupil Personal Recording
RPA	Record of Personal Achievement
RPE	Record of Personal Experience
RPPITB	Rubber and Plastics Processing Industry Training Board
RSA	Royal Society of Arts Examination Board
SCRE	Scottish Council for Research in Education
SWPARP	South Western Profile Assessment Research Project
TVEI	Technical and Vocational Education Initiative
YTS	Youth Training Scheme

Chapter 1

Introduction

The profiles movement shows signs of becoming the most far-reaching and fast growing educational development in recent years. It is possible that it will prove to have been purely a reflex response to massive youth unemployment and the phenomenon of growing numbers of disaffected students within schools – a response which may burgeon and then die.

Alternatively it could provide the doorway through which schools and teachers are led towards a fundamental reappraisal of the curriculum, of assessment procedures and of the patterns of pupil–teacher interaction. Certainly the fact that the Department of Education and Science (DES) has entered the debate to the extent of issuing the Statement of Policy: *Records of achievement* indicates its belief that profiles are here to stay.[1]

The intention of this book is not to attempt a 'hard sell' on behalf of profiles, nor, conversely, to present a picture of such complexity that readers will be dissuaded from ever attempting to profile students. It is, rather, intended to act as a guide through the maze of current developments, to clarify the main issues, to simplify the consideration of alternatives for potential users. It is chiefly intended to offer practical help to those embarking upon the challenge of introducing profiles into their own schools and colleges.

1.1 What is a profile?

A profile is not, in itself, a method of assessment. It is a document which can record assessments of students across a wide range of abilities, including skills, attitudes, personal achievements, personal qualities and subject attainments; it frequently involves the student in its formation, and has a formative as well as a summative function.

This definition identifies elements which might be assessed, including areas beyond those narrow, cognitive skills which traditionally form the basis for assessment. It establishes the principle of student participation, which, while not imperative, is arguably desirable, and it introduces the concept of profiles as tools which may help a formative *process* (see Chapter 4), whilst leading towards a summative end statement. The formative process is the 'profiling' referred to in the title, whilst the summative product is the 'profile'.

The most obvious difference between profiling and traditional reporting is the opportunity which is provided to assess (and by implication to develop) cross-curricular skills, personal qualities and achievements. The great advantage is that profiling looks at the individual and says 'these are the skills and qualities which this person possesses, let's give credit for them, and build on them to develop more skills'. Profiles are able to draw on evidence as alternatives or additions to examination results, and can therefore reflect a wider range of achievements and experiences. A profile offers a fuller, more rounded picture of the individual.

The physical form of a profile can vary from one folded A4 sheet to an elaborate, bound book. With substantial interest in and attention focussed upon profiles, it is increasingly apparent that ideas are developing about what profiles should be: most recent examples are moving away from the brief school report towards something which is central to the learning process.

Profiles can become tools which aid communication between teacher and student, and can form the basis for more detailed record keeping. Profiles can aid the learning and attainments of young people (Chapter 2) by providing them with a continuous record of their achievements, can function as a school-leaving certificate and can provide a source of information for employers and other users.

One of the characteristics of effective profiles is that they should be contributed to by a number of teachers. Sometimes assessments of different teachers are conflated to form an 'average' of submitted comments, but this practice is more likely to produce a blurred, or out of focus, picture rather than the clear, more detailed image which is the aim of profiling. Disagreements between teachers, or between teachers and students, may be settled by discussion and negotiation, but if this fails they can be openly recognised, and are likely to lead to a fairer, more realistic picture than one which is averaged in the interests of expediency.

Another feature central to profiles is the assessment of cross-curricular skills (see Chapter 6), together with the opportunity for the distillation of school subjects into separable elements, which may be separately assessed and which may, as a result, offer a profile of students' attainments *within* a single subject. For example, within mathematics, assessment may be separated into assessment of addition, subtraction, multiplication, division (of whole numbers, fractions and decimals), related thinking, approximations and estimations (see Fig. 1.1).[2] This offers a far more useful aid to diagnosis, with a corresponding opportunity for rectification (see Chapter 2.5) than is provided by a single grade for mathematics.

Inevitably, there is a temptation to ask 'so what's new?'. The answer is, in many cases, 'nothing'. Good teachers already discuss progress with their students; many are aware of the importance of recording personal achievements and of seeing their students as whole people rather than as 'examination fodder'. If there are elements which are new to profiles they can probably be most easily identified in the assessment (and therefore the recognition of the

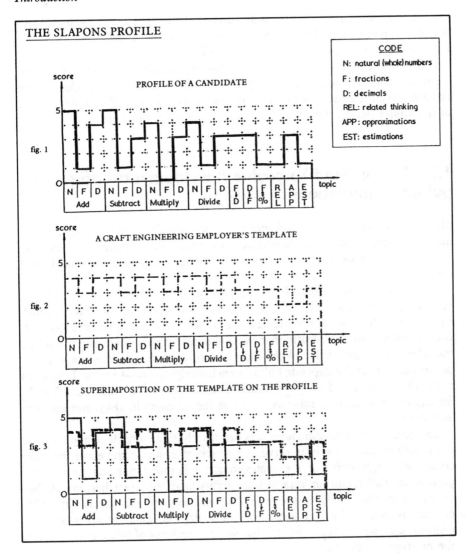

THE SLAPONS PROFILE

CODE
N: natural (whole) numbers
F: fractions
D: decimals
REL: related thinking
APP: approximations
EST: estimations

fig. 1 — PROFILE OF A CANDIDATE

fig. 2 — A CRAFT ENGINEERING EMPLOYER'S TEMPLATE

fig. 3 — SUPERIMPOSITION OF THE TEMPLATE ON THE PROFILE

Fig. 1.1

importance) of cross-curricular skills, and perhaps even more revolutionary, the involvement of students in negotiating their own learning objectives and assessing their own progress (Chapter 2 and Chapter 4).

In the last analysis the main value of profiles is that they draw together all of these varied elements, make explicit for both teachers and students their importance and, under the umbrella of one document, provide a fuller picture of the young person than has hitherto been common practice.

1.2 Background to profile development: critique of public examinations

Much of the unease which has motivated educationists towards the development of profiles stems from dissatisfaction with the public examination system, and, to a lesser degree, with existing reporting procedures in schools and colleges.

It is useful to stand aside from the maelstrom of involvement with day to day preparation of students for examinations and consider the way in which examinations have gradually exerted domination over life in schools today. It is only comparatively recently that examinations have become interwoven into the fabric of society. Prior to the industrial revolution, attendance and qualification at University depended almost exclusively on social status. It was not until 1815 that the first professional examinations were instituted by the Society of Apothecaries, followed by those for solicitors in 1835, and accountants in 1880.

The role of these examinations was not merely to ensure the competence of the practitioners, but also to serve as a means of ensuring the exclusivity and consequent high status of the professional. It is interesting that these three professions still retain an aura of high status, and still erect barriers clothed in mystique which help to preserve a certain mystery and superiority. (One of the reasons why teachers find difficulty in gaining acceptance as professionals may be that everyone has some experience of being at school, and the mystique is dispelled.)

Equally, because these initial examinations *were* associated with high status professions, 'the model of the written theoretical test they used became invested with a similar high status – the status it still retains'.[3]

It is this legacy with which today's schools have been endowed. As a result of these origins, and various other developments in the examination system in the intervening years,[4] the Universities have become invested with considerable influence over the examination system and, as a result, over the curriculum in secondary schools.

A consequence of this phenomenon has been the development of examinations which test the academic abilities of students, and which acknowledge academic excellence to the detriment of the practical, non-cognitive and aesthetic areas of the curriculum. 'This system became the norm of quality control. Its aims were to increase competition, and to select and to reward merit.'[5]

It is this which, I suspect, causes the greatest unease amongst teachers, whose responsibility is to care for the whole student population, and not merely for an elite minority.

a. Elementary education

In the early years of elementary education, when 'the prime purpose of schooling for the poorer classes was to instil moral discipline and social subordination',[6] no provision for external assessment was made for those who did not qualify for the academically able band of pupils. It was not until well after the 1944 Education Act that the 'non-academic' – those classified as suitable for secondary modern education – became drawn into the net of public examinations. Resulting from a combination of parental pressure, prestige-seeking by schools and the desire of young people themselves to acquire certification, more and more people stayed at school to sit an examination at 16+.

b. Certificate of Secondary Education 1963

The Beloe Committee's recommendations that examinations other than GCE 'O' Levels were rationalised resulted in the introduction, in ,1963, of the Certificate of Secondary Education (CSE), offering a greater degree of teacher control and flexibility. CSE was intended to cater for the 40% ability band below the top 20% (destined for GCE).

Twenty years later the demise of CSE was widely predicted – in spite of high hopes and admirable efforts on the part of many teachers. The reality was that on the one hand, the consumer group had been extended so that almost 90% of all pupils took at least one public examination, resulting in two years preparation for exams by many pupils for whom the academic curriculum may not have been the most appropriate. On the other hand, rising unemployment and 'qualification inflation'[7] led to the devaluing of all but the top two grades of CSE – a grade 4, aimed at the 'average' pupil, being regarded by most youngsters as useless. It remains to be seen whether the new General Certificate of Secondary Education (GCSE) will be regarded more highly by sixteen-year-old pupils.

It is then, this history of an examination-oriented society, influenced by professional and university requirements for selecting the most able, which has dominated much of what has happened in schools up to the present day.

c. Arguments in favour of the examination system

It would be easy, particularly in a book on profiles, to lurch to the opposite extreme, to damn all examinations, and propose a total revolution in the current assessment system. I believe that this could result in more damage and confusion than exists at present. It is more helpful to consider the strengths and weaknesses of the present system, and to try to draw upon these findings to suggest improvements. The strengths can be summarised as:

i. Providing achievement 'bench marks' which 'indicate a pupil's success relative to his or her peers. These bench marks enable all those concerned to receive feedback on pupils' progress and achievement.'[8]

ii. Examinations can be seen as a way of increasing social mobility. It was certainly the case that under the old 11+ system youngsters from working class homes who managed to take advantage of grammar school education were sometimes able to move from one social sphere to another. The opportunity existed for young people to 'score' their way out of their own social class.

iii. Examinations have the advantage of being ostensibly 'objective' – the pupil is being externally assessed, and is not exposed to the subjectivity of individual teachers, the risk of personality clash or the effects of teacher expectations on pupil performance.

iv. External examinations can serve as a means of ensuring consistent standards between schools, particularly in a time of growing demand for accountability, and the enforced publication of every school's examination results.

v. The prospect of public examinations looming on the horizon has traditionally acted as a motivating influence for young people in school, with the idea that success in examination leads to a good job.

vi. The examination syllabus facilitates the establishing of learning objectives, and offers a framework within which teachers and students can work.

d. Arguments against the current examination system

i. One of the most over-riding criticisms of examinations has been that they exert a 'straightjacket' upon the curriculum – upon what is taught, and how it is taught. This criticism has recurred in successive reports almost since the inception of public examinations, and is made particularly vociferously at the present time. There is considerable concern at the phenomenon of teachers 'teaching to the exam'.

ii. A second, almost equally strong criticism, which has gained strength particularly in recent years, is the divisive effect which examinations exert within schools and colleges, and within society. Much of the comprehensive ideal appears to be subverted when a substantial percentage of students feel themselves to be second class citizens – either on the basis of not having been selected for GCE examination classes, or, worse still, not having been selected for any examinations.

iii. This 'sheep and goats' effect makes itself felt further in the damage inflicted upon the self-esteem and self-image of pupils, during at least the last two years of compulsory schooling, at a time when their adolescent, developing personalities are at their most vulnerable.

iv. A similar, and allied, phenomenon is brought about by what happens at the *end* of this two year period, when, even with the increased numbers of students sitting for examinations, only 20–30% achieve examination passes which will have credibility in the eyes of users and students. The implication is that 70–80% of the population have failed educationally, an implication which if true would suggest that society is run by illiterate, incapable individuals – an implication which is patently false. It is, moreover, a damning indictment of the education system that so large a proportion of young people are made to feel inadequate and failures by a system which is intended to help, develop and educate all individuals to fulfil their fullest potential.

v. Burgess and Adams make an arresting point when they suggest that examination do not in fact serve well even those in the top 20% for whom the elitist approach is ostensibly intended, as they test narrow cognitive skills, and ignore 'vital human skills and qualities such as an enquiring mind, persistence, co-operation and creativity'.[9]

vi. The corollary to the advantage of objectivity claimed for external examinations is the difficulty in achieving comparability of standards – either in the same subject with different examination boards, in different subjects within the same examination board, or between results in one year compared with another. A common topic of conjecture amongst fourteen to fifteen year olds is which board is 'easiest', and there are grounds for their cynicism. Public attention has recently been focussed on the inequitable effect of the distribution of marks, where a difference of only 13 marks decides whether a candidate achieves a B or a D at 'A' Level – a crucial factor in the determination of life chances.

vii. The obverse side of the coin of the Mortimores' 'bench marks' is the fact that the essentially norm-based nature of examinations leads to large numbers of pupils necessarily 'failing' or achieving low grades in order to satisfy the normal curve of distribution (see Fig. 1.2). The arguments relating to norm-referenced versus criterion-referenced assessment will be discussed more fully in Chapter 4, but one further effect of the norm-based nature of existing examinations is that a paper which may have been judged a pass one year may achieve a lower grade in a subsequent

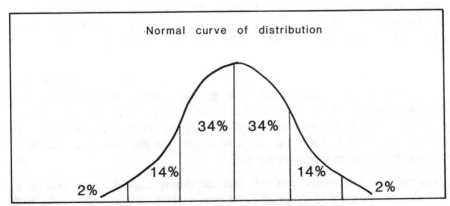

Fig. 1.2

year, in order to conform to the statistical requirements of the normal curve of distribution. There is an unacceptable element of unfairness in such an approach.

viii. The phenomenon of unequal opportunities for the socially disadvantaged is still evidenced in the public examination system which is frequently culturally biased. It is a phenomenon which should be guarded against in order that it is not transferred to any alternative profiling system.

ix. One fact which is frequently overlooked, so firmly are examinations established within the status quo, is their sheer cost. Examination entries amount to a colossal sum when the numbers involved are considered, a factor which may well assume importance in any proposal to substitute, either in whole or in part, profile recording of assessment.

It would be wrong to launch an all-out attack upon the examination system without giving due weight to its advantages, but equally it is important to take account of the major disadvantages.

It is against this background that the introduction of profiles must be considered – it is unrealistic to expect that examinations will be abolished overnight (although we are one of the few western countries retaining so rigid an examination structure at 16+), but it appears clear from the arguments presented in this section that a strong case can be made in favour of developing a more humane and flexible system than that which prevails today.

1.3   The growth of interest in profiles

In spite of these widespread criticisms of the examination system, and the inadequacy of traditional school reports, it was not until the early 1970s that a significant shift towards the development of profiles was discernible.

A number of separate initiatives emerged at this time; one of the first and most influential was heralded by the setting up of a working party under the aegis of the Headmasters' Association of Scotland, and the Scottish Council for Research in Education. The report of this research proved to be a seminal document, and still exerts considerable influence. The working party sought to produce

> for all secondary pupils, a comprehensive picture of their aptitudes and interests so as to enable responsible guidance staff to give them the best possible advice on future curricular and/or vocational choice and on appropriate social and leisure activities; and offering them a common form of statement, which would be generally comprehensible and which would be available to them when appropriate.[10]

After this first major research and development programme related to profiles, the Scottish group produced a profile which was basically a grid, with four levels of competency relating to eight skill areas, which teachers were required to tick. A system for recording these assessments both for individuals and for a whole class was also devised. Many of the profiles developed later were adaptations of this Scottish profile.

Shortly after this the Further Education Unit (FEU) produced the findings of a working party looking into the possibility of rationalising the growing number of pre-employment courses being offered to sixteen to nineteen year olds. This report, which had considerable influence on attitudes and practice in some schools and particularly in colleges, advocated profiling as a more satisfactory method of presenting evidence of the achievements of these young people.[11] Out of this work grew the FEU profile, which was developed in collaboration with City and Guilds to form the basis of the City and Guilds Basic Abilities profile.

At around the same time as the early Scottish initiative, an alternative strategy was being investigated in Wiltshire by Don Stansbury, who developed the Record of Personal Achievement (RPA) scheme, a log-book comprised entirely of pupils' recordings.

During this time there were also pronouncements from established educational bodies – the Schools Council's Working Paper 53 was a major influence,[12] and the DES in Cmnd 6869 questioned 'whether there should be leaving certificates for all pupils'.[13] However, these nationally-based organis-ations promoting pupil profiles would undoubtedly have achieved little more success than earlier calls for reform, had it not been for a considerable growth in the number of individual initiatives. Many schools and colleges to which people now turn for advice (such as Evesham, Clwyd and Comberton) began experimenting with profiles at around the same time as the major Scottish and FEU initiatives. Most of these efforts sprang from a desire within individual organisations to do a better job for pupils and provide them with some sort of worthwhile leaving statement. Many of the most well known profiles have been developed after several false starts, and a 'back to the drawing board' approach.

Much of the development work in profiles has taken place in the post-school sector, and has been encouraged by the FEU. There have been comparatively large-scale projects such as the Clydebank and Humberside initiatives, and interesting work has taken place in individual FE colleges, such as the South East London College, which contributed to development of the RSA numeracy profile, trialled the CGLI basic skills profile, and has undertaken innovative work in the field of computerisation of data.

The Youth Training Scheme (YTS), despite its rapid expansion, the almost frenetic energy with which it was promoted and a certain degree of scepticism regarding its real purpose, has had a considerable effect on attitudes towards profiling in the FE sector, which has, in turn, percolated down to schools.

The aims of YTS are to provide every sixteen-year-old school leaver with one year's training, including off-the-job general education, in order that young people should gain experience and skills which would better equip them for gaining a job, and for coping in the adult world.

It was envisaged at an early stage that a form of assessment different from that previously experienced by youngsters should be utilised. The Manpower Services Commission, vested with power of financing and approving schemes, consequently opted for regular review, and a trainee's log-book of personal experiences and self-assessments, leading to a final profile certificate.

One of the unresolved problems associated with YTS is the question of quality control. In profiling as in every other facet of the scheme there is considerable variation between schemes where the progress review and profile is carried out with a constructive, well organised and systematic approach, resulting in helpful, formative assessment for the student, and those where the process leaves much to be desired. However, there can be little doubt that the imposition of profiling has caused an acceleration in the profiles revolution, and the models of good practice which have undoubtedly been developed are having considerable influence in affecting attitudes towards a new, more comprehensive and hopefully better form of recording assessment.

So far there has been only limited liaison between initiatives in the FE and the schools sector: for example, the RSA refused to allow schools to participate in their Practical Profile Certificate schemes until several determined schools demonstrated that they could not only meet the criteria laid down, but excel. RSA now encourage schools to participate.

Whilst interest in profiles within schools had burgeoned since the late 70s, little systematic information was available about the extent of practice. In 1980, the Schools Council (Programme 5) commissioned a survey of existing profile reports: the results are presented by Janet Balogh,[14] and the widespread degree of interest in this publication demonstrated the need for more information and guidance.

In contrast to supposed interest, it appeared that only twenty-five schools in the country were actually operating pupil profiles. Perhaps part of this paradox lies in the difficulty already mentioned, of the diversity of titles and activities which come under the one generic term 'profile', and hence other schools may have been operating schemes which conformed to the spirit yet still fell outside the definition of 'profile'. More likely, however, is the difficulty of transforming general interest into practical programmes within schools.

The extent of the explosion of interest can be illustrated by comparing Balogh's twenty-five schools in 1980 with a recent survey carried out by Evesham High School (one of Balogh's examples) in February 1983. At that time over 200 schools from 50 LEAs had made individual enquiries about the Evesham PAR. The school carried out a survey and discovered that of the 50% who replied, at least 43% had set up a profile scheme, 43% were considering it, and only 18% had rejected it after consideration. [15]

There is little doubt that the strength of the profiles movement, and the impetus for its growth, have come from the grass roots involvement of groups of teachers and schools working together. This has, in many cases, been built upon at local authority level, with Education Authorities such as Avon, Dorset,

Somerset, Coventry and Oxford seconding teachers to investigate and develop profiling within their counties.

1.4 Why profiles?

It is well worth considering *why* profiles should have gained such prominence within a comparatively short space of time – they have almost acquired the status of being a 'boom industry' in a time of general economic recession, of falling rolls and of widespread contraction within the education system. The paradox is intriguing, yet it could be that the growth of profiles is not so much a paradox as a direct result of these factors, together with the marked increase in youth unemployment.

There is increasing evidence that people are beginning to ask what they are being assessed for, and calling into question the whole purpose of education.

Briefly, the main reasons why profiles appear to be receiving the attention and sustained effort which is being devoted to their development include:

i. Growing dissatisfaction with traditional public examinations which disenfranchise a large percentage of young people.

ii. The belief that all pupils should leave school with a worthwhile statement of documentary evidence relating to their time in school.

iii. Interest in recognising and assessing areas of achievement beyond those encapsulated in cognitive learning.

iv. The provision of more comprehensive information for users (employers, further and higher education, careers service, etc.).

v. The influence of the MSC and the 17+ CPVE examination.

vi. Acceptance of the ability of profiles to emphasise good points rather than to record failure.

vii. The use of assessment methods to help diagnosis of student strengths and weaknesses, and to build on this, bringing assessment into the centre of the curriculum.

viii. Growing awareness of the ability to motivate pupils, and to enhance their self-awareness by involving them in the preparation of profiles.

ix. Belief that profiles may help to combat the disaffection of potentially disruptive pupils by encouraging interest in student participation in assessment, involving a negotiated pattern of student–teacher learning and the setting of achievable goals.

x. Recognition of the possibility of profile assessment acting as a tool for staff development, and for improving teacher skills in assessment.

xi. Awareness of the implications for the whole curriculum in a new form of integrated learning/assessment procedure.[16]

All of these considerations converged at a time when mass structural unemployment, increasingly disaffected youth in schools and colleges, qualification inflation, the influence of MSC, the new CPVE and the movement seeking to broaden the curriculum all contributed towards producing a climate which was receptive to new proposals for profiling.

1.5   Some recent developments

The explosion of interest in profiles referred to in 1.3 has borne fruit in a number of initiatives which have extended beyond individual organisations or consortia of organisations. Some examples include:

a.   The Oxford Certificate of Educational Achievement (OCEA)

In the summer of 1982 the Oxfordshire Education Authority, the University of Oxford Department of Educational Studies and the Oxford Delegacy of Local Examinations discussed the development of an alternative method of crediting and rewarding the achievements of young people.

It was proposed that such an alternative could consist of:

P component: (personal record) which will consist of a personal record made by the student, based upon formative experiences both within and beyond the curriculum. Its intention is formative, and it is aimed at the self-development of the individual.

G component: which consists of graded assessments of achievements within the curriculum.

E component: which consists of a record of all external examination results.

This proposal broadens the scope of traditional examinations to encompass both graded tests in some subjects (such as English, Mathematics, Science and Modern Languages) akin to the mastery learning involved in music examinations. The second innovative element in the certificate is the inclusion of the 'P' component.

In addition to the originators of the scheme, three further LEAs (Somerset, Leicestershire and Coventry) joined the development scheme, each investing significantly in terms of full-time teacher secondments to the project.

A two year pilot programme began in 1985; the Certificate is due to be offered nationwide in 1987.

This collaborative initiative has excited widespread interest and has been influential in encouraging decision-makers to take profiling seriously (the recommendations of the DES[17] closely resemble the format devised by OCEA).

b.   South Western Profile Assessment Research Project (SWPARP)

This initiative, instigated as a result of collaboration between the South Western Examinations Board, Bath University, Avon, Gloucestershire, Wiltshire, Devon, Somerset and Cornwall LEAs, and with contributions from the Department of Education and Science and the Secondary Examinations Council, has adopted a different perspective.

In contrast to the Oxford proposal to develop and market a specific package, SWPARP is intended to provide much needed research and evidence on the effects of profiles on

(a) The teaching content and approach in subjects, with the longer term effect upon the philosophy of the school. This implies a system which will be a mixture of cross-curricular skills and qualities which can be included and assessed meaningfully in the formative situation and can be reported upon acceptably in the summative.
(b) Resources. Teacher time and commitment within schools and the consequent implications for the Local Education Authorities in staffing, materials and in-service training in making the Profile available for all pupils.
(c) The effect of a Profile Assessment system on existing pastoral structures within a school.
(d) The ways in which pupils can participate in terms of self-assessment and the part which can be played by the pupil in a 'negotiated curriculum'.
(e) The potential difficulties in combining the needs of summative assessment with the requirements of the formative process. Whilst it is considered that the latter are the more important, it is accepted that assessment and curriculum go hand in hand and that reporting and acceptability to users must not be overlooked.[18]

Fourteen schools throughout the south west of England were invited to participate in the project. This initiative provides the first opportunity for the objective evaluation of a variety of different profile schemes, their merits, drawbacks and unforeseen implications, and should provide a useful source of data for embarking upon the development of profiling schemes.

c. Welsh profile
In November 1983 the Schools Council Committee for Wales produced a discussion paper incorporating a draft proposal for a Welsh profile.[19]

Leaning heavily upon the work already undertaken in the Clwyd pilot profile scheme, a working party set up under the auspices of the Committee for Wales, the Schools Council and the Welsh Joint Education Committee was instituted in November 1980. Fifteen pilot schools participated and twelve further schools were involved in an advisory capacity. At the end of the piloting period, the first report suggested that 'the study had established the feasibility of introducing a nationally *available* profile' and a draft profile based upon the 'comment bank' approach was offered for use, whilst still being subject to further development.

The Welsh profile is unique in that it is the first *national* profile to be made available. It was a bold venture, perhaps made easier by the fact that the Welsh Education system is more amenable to a centralised approach than that of England or N. Ireland; a joint GCE and CSE Examination Board controls the examination system, and its area of jurisdiction is more compact geographically. However, the progress made by this venture will provide invaluable lessons for development of profiles in the rest of the United Kingdom.

d. Northern Record of Achievement (NRA)

In 1983 the five examining boards of the Northern Examination Association (Associated Lancashire Schools Examining Board, Joint Matriculation Board, North Regional Examinations Board, North West Regional Examinations Board, Yorkshire and Humberside Regional Examinations Board) and the LEAs of Bradford, Gateshead, Leeds, Manchester, Rotherham, Wakefield and Wigan established a steering group to consider the possibility of introducing records of achievement.

In July 1984 a newsheet outlined progress,[20] and announced that the record would have three main elements:

i. public examination results
ii. other evidence of academic attainment
iii. information about the pupil's personal characteristics and achievements.

This framework bears a close resemblance to that of the OCEA initiative, and reflects the DES's recommendations that pilot schemes should be based upon collaboration between examination boards and LEAs and should include these three areas.

One characteristic of this project is the speed with which piloting was launched – participating LEAs began piloting in selected schools in September 1984, in contrast to OCEA with its two year development programme.

Another interesting characteristic is the NRA's proposal to introduce 'unit accreditation' and 'credit accumulation'. This is based upon the principle of breaking down the curriculum into small units which can be assessed and credited as students progress, and which can be progressive, covering all ability levels. This system is still in the early stages of development, but it can be seen that it could well provide a useful motivating factor in student learning.

e. Technical and Vocational Education Initiative (TVEI)

One of the national initiatives which promises to be a significant factor in the development of profiling is TVEI.

Launched in November 1982 under the auspices of MSC, TVEI was seen by many as a threat to the autonomy enjoyed by education. The lavish funding of MSC, and the creation of Youth Training Schemes, had already caused some concern, but TVEI heralded the intrusion of MSC into schools as well as colleges. Despite this initial concern, and the reservations of many about the desirability of introducing pre-vocational education at the age of fourteen and the possibly divisive nature of such an innovation, sixty-six of the ninety-six LEAs made submissions to participate in the initial pilot scheme consisting of schools in fourteen LEAs. Although there is a vocational orientation, students are also encouraged to enter for traditional examinations.

One of the criteria laid down for schools and colleges participating in TVEI is that students should have profiles recording their progress and achievement.

This inevitably resulted in some institutions hurriedly adapting 'off the shelf models' whilst others preferred to design profiles to fit their specific course.

f. Certificate of Pre-vocational Education (CPVE)

The CPVE arose from a DES initiative seeking to rationalise the plethora of non-'A' level courses available to young people over sixteen, offering in one package a form of certification which will be valued by young people and recognised by employers. It provides a framework and guidelines incorporating a range of objectives, with recommendations for good practice.

During 1984–5, fifteen pilot schemes in operation offered certification for CPVE. The aims are to provide

i. continued general education, through a vocational focus
ii. career/job training, with mandatory work experience or job-sampling
iii. transition to adult and working life.

Profiling is an integral part of the assessment procedure for CPVE (see Fig. 1.3). It is interesting that in both the MSC-sponsored and the DES-sponsored initiatives into pre-vocational education profiling should be given prominence. The combination of these two recommendations means that profiling will actually take place in schools and colleges, which could have the effect of spreading profiling to the rest of the school population.

g. DES Statement of Policy: *Records of achievement*

The final major new initiative in the field has been the DES Statement issued in July 1984, illustrating the fact that the profiles movement really has been a 'bottom-up' rather than a 'top-down' model for curriculum innovation.

The Statement draws together many of the concerns and priorities of those involved in the development of profiling, emphasising particularly that profiles, or 'Records of achievement' should fulfil the following purposes:

(i) Recognition of achievement. Records and recording systems should recognise, acknowledge and give credit for what pupils have achieved and experienced, not just in terms of results in public examinations, but in other ways as well. They should do justice to pupils' own efforts and to the efforts of teachers, parents, ratepayers and taxpayers to give them a good education.

(ii) Motivation and personal development. They should contribute to pupils' personal development and progress by improving their motivation, providing encouragement and increasing their awareness of strengths, weaknesses and opportunities.

(iii) Curriculum and organisation. The recording process should help schools to identify the all-round potential of their pupils and to consider how well their curriculum, teaching and organisation enable pupils to develop the general, practical and social skills which are to be recorded.

(iv) A document of record. Young people leaving school or college should take with them a short summary document of record which is recog-

CORE AREA 3 - COMMUNICATION

FACTOR	REF NO	CORE COMPETENCE STATEMENT	OBJECTIVE REFERENCE
36 WRITING	36.1	Can write legibly	4.1-4.2 5.8
	36.2	Can convey straight-forward information and ideas in writing	
	36.3	Can select and use an appropriate style and form of writing to maintain the confidence of the user	
	36.4	Can create and organise written material in a style suited to the purpose	
37 CRITICAL APPROACH TO COMMUNICATION	37.1	Can recognise ambiguous statements	5.1-5.3
	37.2	Can make critical judgements of ambiguous statements	
38 SECOND/FOREIGN LANGUAGE	38.1	Can recognise and use a few words of a second/foreign language	5.9-5.10
	38.2	Can communicate well in a second/foreign language	
39 EVALUATION	39.1	Can recognise success or failure in communication and take appropriate action	5.12

Note: Reading of charts, diagrams and drawings is covered under Aim 2.2 of Numeracy.

Fig. 1.3: A profile for CPVE

nised and valued by employers and institutions of further and higher education. This should provide a more rounded picture of candidates for jobs or courses than can be provided by a list of examination results, thus helping potential users to decide how candidates could be best employed, or for which jobs, training schemes or courses they are likely to be suitable.[21]

Added impetus is given to the movement by the allocation of funds for piloting development projects, which will be monitored by the DES.

The Secretaries of State called, in this Statement of Policy, for the mounting of between five and ten pilot schemes over a period of three years, to explore a variety of issues including

- the purposes of records and the recording system;
- the target group;
- the treatment of personal achievements and qualities;
- the presentation of examination results and other evidence of educational attainment;
- national currency and accreditation;
- recording processes, including the relationship with existing reporting systems.[22]

The initial Draft Statement of Policy produced a flood of criticisms at the lack of emphasis on the formative process of profiling: this was adjusted in the final document.

Some reservations may be expressed at the prominent positions of examination boards in pilot schemes, leading to fears that the criteria will lead merely to the substitution of a new curriculum straightjacket in place of the existing model.

The fact that in a time of financial stringency and contraction in the education service the DES has agreed to finance such pilot projects is an indication of the increasing credibility being accorded to the profile movement, and is a recognition of the work undertaken by committed individuals to date. The outcome of these pilot schemes will undoubtedly prove to be a watershed for the whole profiling movement, while the suggestion that *all* secondary schools should offer a school leaving certificate by 1990 affords added impetus to the development of profiles.

Summary

This chapter has established the terms of reference in this book governing what is meant by a profile. It has sought to identify those areas in which assessments may be recorded, the difference between profiles and traditional examinations and some of the ways in which the sensitive use of a profile might offer an improvement upon the old system.

It has sought to trace the development of the profile movement, commencing with a critique of the examination system, leading into a more detailed consideration of the sudden explosion of interest, examining some of the major profiling initiatives and culminating in the Secretary of State's Statement of Policy (July 1984).

Notes

1. Department of Education and Science, and Welsh Office, *Records of achievement: a statement of policy*, 1984.
2. Shell Centre of Mathematical Education, University of Nottingham, *School leavers' attainment profile of numerical skills (SLAPONS)*, reproduced from Further Education Unit, *Profiles*, 1982.
3. Broadfoot, P., *Assessment, schools and society*, Methuen, 1979.
4. For a more detailed account of the development of public examinations, see Mortimore, P. and Mortimore, J., *Secondary school examinations; helpful servants or dominating master?* Bedford Way Papers No. 18, University of London Institute of Education, 1983.
5. *Ibid.*
6. *Ibid.*
7. Dore, R., *The diploma disease*, Allen and Unwin, 1976.
8. Mortimore and Mortimore, *Secondary school examinations*.
9. Burgess, T. and Adams, E. (eds.), *Outcomes of education*, Macmillan, 1980.
10. Scottish Council for Research in Education, *Pupils in profiles*, Hodder and Stoughton, 1977.
11. Further Education Unit, *A basis for choice*, 1979.
12. Schools Council, *The whole curriculum 13 to 16*, Working Paper 53, 1975.
13. Department of Education and Science, *Education in schools: a consultative document*, Cmnd 6869, HMSO, 1977.
14. Balogh, Janet, *Profile reports for school leavers*, Longman for Schools Council, 1982.
15. Bowring, Malcolm, *Pupil profile development in schools*, Education and Industry Centre, Worcester College of Higher Education, 1983.
16. Hitchcock, Gloria, *Profiles*, Avon Education Authority, 1984.
17. Department of Education and Science, and Welsh Office, *Records of achievement*.
18. South Western Profile Assessment Research Project, *South Western Profile Assessment Research Project*, South Western Examinations Board, 1984.
19. Schools Council Committee for Wales, *Profile reporting in Wales*, 1983.
20. Northern Examining Association, *A northern record of achievement* 1984.
21. Department of Education and Science, and Welsh Office, *Records of achievement*.
22. *Ibid.*

Chapter 2

Purposes

To a great extent this chapter on 'purposes' can be related to the earlier section asking 'why profiles?' (1.4). Many of the purposes are an attempt to satisfy the concerns of both practitioners and theoretical educationists, and include the desire of teachers, local authorities and latterly the DES to fulfil some of the following functions:

2.1 Improve student motivation.

2.2 Aid discipline.

2.3 Increase communication and improve relationships.

2.4 Contribute to pastoral work (guidance, counselling, getting to know oneself better).

2.5 Aid diagnosis

2.6 Aid staff development.

2.7 Improve selection.

In addition to these purposes which are examined in detail, additional purposes, which are discussed elsewhere in the book, include the wish to: improve recording and reporting (1.4); to offer a worthwhile leaving certificate (1.4); to make opportunities for self and peer assessment (3.2); to place assessment at the centre of the learning process (4.2); and to free the curriculum (4.4). However, profiles which are narrowly focussed will not achieve these effects.

2.1 Motivation

One of the most important features of profiles is their potential ability to motivate young people.

In this context 'motivation' is defined as stimulating the interest of a person in order that he/she will work harder, with more satisfaction – not merely in the field of academic attainment, although improved attainment may well result, but also in participation in the whole range of activities available in school or college. It is the development of an inner drive, an integral part of the individual, which will encourage the student to set targets, and to persevere until those targets are reached – whether in academic, sporting, social or personal development. To be really lasting, such motivation needs to be intrinsic, and not merely the attempt to satisfy some extrinsic goal. The prizes attached to the targets may be external, but they may equally be internal prizes such as enhanced feelings of self-worth.

The DES Statement of Policy recognises the importance of motivating young people when it says 'they [records of achievement] should contribute to pupils' personal development and progress by improving their motivation'.[1]

This purpose is given prominence by the DES, although little attempt is made to elaborate on precisely how or why profiles improve motivation. The belief that they *can* improve motivation is, however, supported by practising teachers experienced in profiling.

In a range of schools studied, individual teachers made comments such as: 'since we introduced profiling the kids' motivation has certainly improved'. This in no way represents objective research evidence, but the belief was widespread. Students in the same institutions generally supported the view that profiles improved their motivation, although the response was not unanimous. A group of students in one school agreed with a youth who remarked: 'It would have been better if we'd had profiles in the Fourth year – it gives you something to aim for.' A fifteen year old remarked: 'If you have a target, a certain amount of motivation is needed to reach it. Profiles help to increase motivation because they help you to believe you can reach the target you set yourself.'

Those who are sceptical of the potential benefits of profiles argue that examinations already stimulate motivation, particularly in the case of the more academically able. This is undoubtedly true, but there are also a great many young people who do not respond to this stimulus. It is also true that even among the academic elite, feelings of failure are frequently prevalent. It is not uncommon for students with three or four 'O' levels to feel that they have 'failed'. One youngster even said 'If I don't get an "A" in English I'll feel that I've failed.'

It is the competitive, norm-referenced nature of examinations which nourishes negative self-image and disheartens so many young people in school and college. While it is recognised that in the foreseeable future examinations will continue to play an important part in the lives of students, profiles emerge as an attempt to alleviate some of the preoccupation with success and failure, and to provide students with an alternative, more sensitive yardstick against which to measure themselves, and which it is hoped will instil a new motivation.

So what exactly is different about profiles? Why should they motivate? Part of the answer must surely lie in the different ethos surrounding profiles – an ethos which encourages and emphasises co-operation rather than competition. For example, one school dedicated to the concept of profiles specifically encourages active group work in all subjects, and has abandoned all internal competitive examinations.

This emphasis on recognising achievement rather than reinforcing failure is another powerful factor in profiles' potential for motivating students. The recognition of achievement – whether academic, musical, sporting, caring or just the ability to hold down a part-time job – is the essence of the profiling philosophy. It may be that the achievements are far from spectacular; one of the advantages of giving formal credit for a wide range of activities is that youngsters may be encouraged to view as worthwhile some of the achievements which have hitherto appeared to them to be of little value. Even small advances can be recognised and accredited, and the dual functions of recognising achievement and giving credit for success are valuable ingredients in stimulating motivation.

Part of the philosophy underpinning the profiles movement is the requirement that *good* points should be emphasised, and that the attributes and achievements of individuals should be recorded in constructive terms. One of the outcomes of this approach is that increased confidence may lead to improved performance.

It has long been possible for students possessing qualities or attainments lying outside the established structure of accreditation to go unrecognised. For example, school-based work experience produces many examples of young people labelled as difficult and disruptive being transformed into reliable, sensible, helpful individuals in the work situation. All too often this has been seen as peripheral to the reporting system; formal credit for a very real achievement has been slight or non-existent.

Under a system of profiles, or records of achievement, an explicit policy of recognition of good points obligates the institution to seek out and give full credit for all achievements, and to provide opportunities for a range of achievements to be experienced.

The DES recognises the importance of adopting a positive approach when it says: 'assessments should concentrate on concrete evidence of positive qualities such as enthusiasm, enterprise, etc. . . . ', and 'the final document of record should not refer to failure or defects'.[2]

This does not mean that the whole profiling process should be a bland diet of platitudes. It would be disregarded by pupils, teachers and users who would be quick to recognise a 'snow job' if it was filled with meaningless praise. Discussion of negative characteristics and evidence of poor standards of behaviour or attainment are a vital part of the formative profiling process. Nevertheless, this belongs in the process, and not in the final product.

The importance of positive reinforcement in the stimulation of motivation is illustrated in the example of one school where a pile of unwanted CSE certificates await collection. In contrast, there is not one school-leaving certificate to be seen. The certificate is a simple A4 sheet – the Head attributes the high value placed upon it by the pupils as stemming from the fact that it is a positive statement of their achievements.

Once again this is not a revolutionary philosophy. Education has always been intended as a means of encouraging students, and many, many good teachers struggle to put the philosophy into practice, but the constraints imposed by the competitive examination system (which inevitably implies winners and losers) ensure that the struggle is often in vain. The advantage of profiles is that by making explicit the emphasis upon positive acts, attainments and attributes regardless of the peer group norm, a far more constructive approach to the individual's self-development is made possible.

One obvious question arising from discussion of motivation is 'why motivate them? What's the point – is it just to keep the trouble makers in line?'. The answer must surely be not simply that it is necessary to motivate students in order to improve their academic attainment, although this is certainly a valid objective. It is that with increased motivation triggered by the recognition of positive achievements which may hitherto have passed unnoticed, or have been recognised only within a particular lesson or activity, and which are now given status and importance, the individual's feelings of self-worth are enhanced. Pervasive feelings of failure may be replaced by positive feelings, leading to an overall improvement in self-image and self-esteem. In other words, the individuals are encouraged to feel better about themselves, to see both small and large achievements as really having meaning, and they may *work* better.

The word 'encouraged' is important in this context – one youngster said: 'profiles can encourage you in the things you are doing well, it would be nice to be told when you are doing well, it could change your attitude and help you get better in the things you're not doing well'.

The mere physical presence of a profile record or a profiling system will not, of course, provide an instantaneous, magical enhancement of self-esteem. It is dependent upon an inter-related pastoral support system recognising this as a worthy aim, and it also depends upon what is to be profiled.

Finally, a convincing answer to the question 'why motivate?' must be that the processes of recognising achievement, of recording and reporting in positive terms, of constructively emphasising good points, of learning to experience success rather than failure and of developing enhanced feelings of self-worth and self-esteem almost inevitably lead to increased self-confidence. It would seem to be a worthwhile end to produce young people with the ability to lead independent lives with greater confidence in their own abilities.

To summarise, profiles offer both short-term and long-term benefits if they can increase motivation. In the short term, increased motivation can lead to greater interest and participation in school life, producing students with improved self-confidence and enhanced self-worth. In the long term this should lead to self-reliant individuals better able to make their way in the adult world.

2.2 Aid discipline

There are two separate, yet related, facets of profiles as agents of social control. The negative aspect is considered in the 'pitfalls' section (5.2).

However, the potential of profiles as a means of channelling and defusing the frustration and anger of many young people seems, to many teachers, to be a legitimate and desirable function. Teachers are seeking additional methods of coping with the growing numbers of disaffected youngsters; seeing profiles as an aid to discipline is really an extension of the concept of profiles as motivators.

A number of teachers commented on the possibility of reducing problems caused by disruptive, 'switched-off' pupils: almost without exception they viewed it as a thoroughly laudable aim. For many it was the principal reason for becoming involved with profiles at all (Chapter 1).

The growth in youth unemployment, qualification inflation and the consequent devaluation of examination certificates has reduced the effectiveness of the 'carrot' of examinations as the passport to success, leading to widespread disillusionment. The corresponding reduction in the effectiveness of the threat of examination failure if pupils do not work hard and conform has removed the 'stick' for those not wholeheartedly devoted to the pursuit of academic excellence.

Indiscipline in the classroom may be associated with this phenomenon, or it may more accurately be ascribed to wider changes in society as a whole. Whether the underlying cause in specific instances is identified with either of these possibilities, or with the many other possible reasons, classroom teachers are facing increasing pressures.

Hargreaves suggests that a teacher with discipline problems 'has in some way failed to master the task of creating order in his classroom', and suggests that part of the reason for this may be the teacher's failure to define the situation in his/her own terms, and to establish dominance in the classroom.[3]

This may well be true, but many teachers argue that it is becoming increasingly difficult to define the situation in their own terms. One of the reasons for many idealistic, concerned teachers facing rejection and 'discipline problems' is that unless schools are reorganised radically, 'pupils are unlikely to find school rewarding for most of the time'.[4]

It would be far too simplistic to argue that universal implementation of vibrant, exciting lessons, interesting to all pupils at all times, would solve the problem of indiscipline at a stroke. It is reasonable, however, to believe that moves already afoot in many individual institutions and in some LEAs to instigate radical reappraisal of the curriculum should facilitate the introduction of curricula which many students would consider more relevant to their needs. Much of this reappraisal has been triggered by initiatives in the field of pre-vocational education. The relationship of profiles to the curriculum will be discussed in Chapter 4, but it is clear that, taken in conjunction with curriculum reform, the involvement of students in their own assessment offers an opportunity to counter the justified claim that all too often schools are simply not sufficiently interesting to engage students' commitment.

Illustrating this point, one teacher contemplating the introduction of profiles saw a clear relationship between methods of assessment and disruptive behaviour. She said: 'We set them targets they can't possibly achieve and they inevitably react by playing up. If we involve them, and help them to achieve success they should feel far more commitment to what they're doing.'

In this way it is possible, and in the experience of many teachers who have implemented a profile system it actually does work, that those aspects of a profiling system which help to trigger motivation may be further mobilised to counteract disruptive disillusionment experienced by many teenagers today, so that they may be offered a diet which is more attractive and more digestible.

In addition to the disaffected pre-sixteen students, education needs to provide opportunities for the 'enforced' stayers-on to test out their adult roles. This opportunity used to be provided by work: being given responsibility for one's own learning helps.

2.3 Increase communication and improve relationships

Increased communication, resulting in improved relationships between pupils and teachers is another great bonus offered by profiles. In the early days, most schools and colleges introducing profiles concentrated on the summative function – little systematic consideration had been given to the formative side.

In visiting schools, talking to teachers and pupils, it was significant that in every case, at some stage, teachers remarked 'one of the spin-offs is that I've come to know the pupils better'. This was rarely one of the expressed intentions of the school, and it was not on my original list of points for investigation. The frequency with which it occurred indicates that the improved knowledge and communication – 'I certainly talk to the pupils more' – was a direct result of teachers being asked to look at pupils' personality, achievements and needs in a much more systematic way.

It is now becoming more widely accepted that increased communication should be built into the profiling process, and can lead to an all-round improvement in relationships. Another common remark was: 'Yes, profiles are a lot of work, but they're worth it just in terms of reduced hassle.'

Another remark reflecting this belief was made by a teacher who said 'I'm not claiming that all our problems are solved by profiling, but the school certainly seems a happier place.'

It is a logical outcome of increased levels of communication that relationships will improve – not inevitable, but likely. In the first place, young people in school or college value and respond to being treated as individuals – one youngster said: 'I like profiles because the teachers seem more interested in you as a person', whilst another said: 'You get to know the teachers better.'

The unique feature of formative profiling is that it actually demands one to one communication – it is no longer possible to treat a class as one entity. This was a principle endorsed by the Avon Working Party, when it wrote in, and thereby formalised, the necessity for youngsters to participate and collaborate in the preparation of their profiles.[5]

I do not claim that this approach is 100% beneficial; there may still be antagonism and non-co-operation, and problems may arise from the need for teachers to adopt a new approach, to develop counselling skills, or simply because in a new, open approach in the words of one teacher: 'You sometimes hear things you simply can't handle – either about other staff or about the child's private life.'

Nevertheless, it appears to me that anything which can help to break down the barriers between teacher and taught is a worthwhile exercise.

Perhaps the key to this phenomenon lies in the equation 'increased communication = increased understanding = improved relationships'.

2.4 Contribute to pastoral work (guidance, counselling, getting to know oneself better)

The profiling process is inextricably linked with the pastoral system within the school. The pastoral function is bound up with guidance and counselling of students. The essence of the formative approach to profiling lies in the improvement of pupil attainment, allied to increased interaction and improved communication between teacher and taught.

It is obvious that there are significant implications both for the pastoral system and for tutors working within that system. One benefit which profiling may offer to existing pastoral care systems is that the pastoral curriculum is made more visible. As realisation dawns that skills needed for profiling may already be found within the pastoral set-up, so other teachers may be made aware of the importance of the work undertaken by the pastoral team, and the value of pastoral work. Not only does a strong pastoral system help ease the introduction of profiles, conversely the widespread interest in, and acceptance of, the inevitability of profiles can enhance and strengthen the work of the pastoral team, including the members of the careers department and the social education department. Within the careers department, for example, self-assessment and the setting of realistic individual targets have long been part of the programme.

Equally, the role of social education is closely akin to the effective, formative part of personal recording, concerned with helping individuals to know themselves better. The growth of developmental group work has helped to create a favourable climate within those schools which have embraced it. Many teachers feel threatened by the exposed, open position in which they find themselves on the introduction of profiles. Active tutorial work can help to break down those barriers. Active tutorial work is essentially concerned with active participatory teaching and learning methods which can change the quality of relationships between teacher and student.

In one school, which was about to introduce a system of profiling, the preliminary three years' group tutorial work had established a climate in which profiles would sit easily alongside existing practice. This had not been achieved painlessly, but by the systematic training of a large number of staff, with the initial core of trained teachers undertaking the training of others. In a situation where the groundwork has been laid, profiles should sit easily alongside existing pastoral structures to the mutual benefit of both, in an atmosphere where respect for the individual, and individual interaction, are already part of the ethos of the school.

Reviewing papers developed by CCDU illustrate the close relationship between the aims of profiling, student reviewing and tutorial work.[6]

  i. To increase learners' confidence in staff as they come to appreciate how well the staff know them, their abilities and potential.
 ii. To increase learners' confidence in themselves by learning what they have achieved and how well they are doing.
iii. To increase learners' motivation by allowing them to participate fully in decisions about their programmes of work.
 iv. To increase learners' ability to give and receive feedback about their experience, performance and satisfaction with their programmes of work.

An example of the way in which profiling has implications for the social education programme was highlighted by one teacher who said

> The questions asked in the personal qualities section of the profile could be taken entirely from the social education syllabus. I could usefully build a whole term's work around these questions. For example, 'how much do I take on something to do, and do it as well as I can without being checked up on?' could lead to some really penetrating discussions.

The necessary negotiation skills are not possessed by all teachers, and some will be either unwilling or unable to acquire them. Nevertheless, the inter-relationship between profiles and the pastoral system offers the opportunity to extend both awareness and training to a far greater proportion of the teaching population than ever before. Tutors need negotiation skills not only in their dealings with pupils, but in their dealings with other teachers. The concept of profiling, involving as it does assessments from a range of teachers, frequently requires collation by the tutor. I have witnessed a sensitive, skilled tutor faced with the task of having to go back to teachers and say: 'I don't think we can really say this about Jim on a summative profile, do you? Shall we have another look at it and see if there is a more constructive way of putting it?'

The same applies to the renegotiation of assessments with pupils. There is, however, one problem associated with the issue of renegotiation with colleagues. The young tutor, faced with the task of persuading the Deputy Head to adopt a different approach, is confronted by a very difficult task indeed.

This is a problem which would be eased by recognising it *before* implementing profiles, rather than allowing it to emerge in a random way. Perhaps a mechanism can then be devised within the school to cope with such difficulties. There is little doubt that the problem will arise: whilst in the early, pilot stages collating tutors may be sufficiently senior for the problem to be averted, with wholesale implementation, all tutors, some of them very junior, will be involved. On the other hand, the increased liaison could result in an improvement in the quality of *teacher* relationships.

Asking teachers to assess pupils across a whole range of skills, where previously they may have been concerned only with their subject, introduces a new element: they frequently recognise the value of the support available from the pastoral system, and take advantage of it. This has further repercussions in helping to break down the barriers of the academic/pastoral divide, which is still a common feature of some schools.

Hopefully, the result of this is to extend a humanising individualising approach beyond the confines of the tutor period, to affect the whole life of the school.

2.5 Aid diagnosis

Diagnostic assessment differs from much of the assessment carried out in schools, which is predominantly summative, designed to report and pass judgement on students' attainments.

Diagnosis involves establishing the individual's strengths and weaknesses, either within discrete subjects or in cross-curricular skills. It is also concerned with the identification of learning difficulties and agendas, with the explicit aim of taking appropriate remedial action.

Satterly states that there are two main approaches to diagnostic assessment:[7]
  i. to locate the relative weakness or 'malfunctioning' of the child's perceptual or intellectual process
 ii. to infer the nature of intellectual processes hidden from view to the outside observer.

I would suggest that a third approach can usefully be added to these two:
iii. to identify specific areas of existing or potential strength and interest in the individual.

The first approach is concerned with formal tests designed to analyse students' performance in a specific skill, and to identify areas of difficulty within each category. There is a wide variety of such tests which can be administered (perhaps the most familiar relate to mathematics and reading), and which produce a range of 'objective' statistical scores. These scores may, in themselves, be recorded in the form of a 'profile'.

Inherent in the administration of such tests is the assumption that remedial action is available. One example of this approach to diagnostic assessment is illustrated in Fig. 2.1.

Satterly's second category adopts a far less formal approach to diagnosis. It involves the informal judgements of teachers based upon their day to day contact with students. The teacher has far greater flexibility in interpreting students' difficulties (a more detailed account of this approach can be found

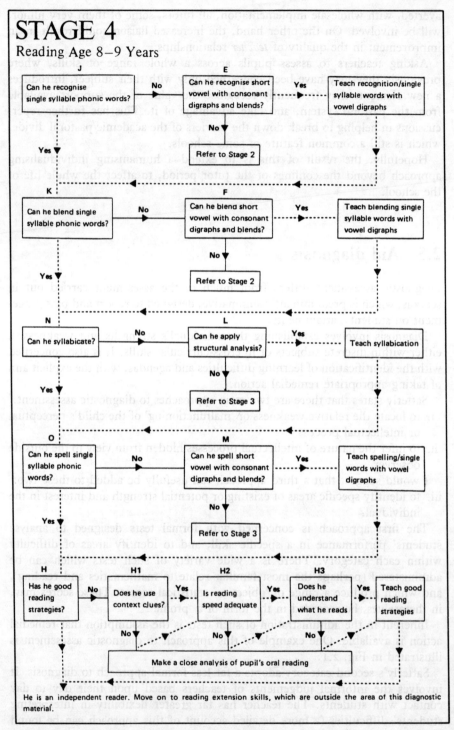

STAGE 4
Reading Age 8–9 Years

J — Can he recognise single syllable phonic words? — **No** → **E** — Can he recognise short vowel with consonant digraphs and blends? — **Yes** → Teach recognition/single syllable words with vowel digraphs

No ↓ Refer to Stage 2

K — Can he blend single syllable phonic words? — **No** → **F** — Can he blend short vowel with consonant digraphs and blends? — **Yes** → Teach blending single syllable words with vowel digraphs

No ↓ Refer to Stage 2

N — Can he syllabicate? — **No** → **L** — Can he apply structural analysis? — **Yes** → Teach syllabication

No ↓ Refer to Stage 3

O — Can he spell single syllable phonic words? — **No** → **M** — Can he spell short vowel with consonant digraphs and blends? — **Yes** → Teach spelling/single words with vowel digraphs

No ↓ Refer to Stage 3

H — Has he good reading strategies? — **No** → **H1** — Does he use context clues? — **Yes** → **H2** — Is reading speed adequate — **Yes** → **H3** — Does he understand what he reads — **Yes** → Teach good reading strategies

Make a close analysis of pupil's oral reading

He is an independent reader. Move on to reading extension skills, which are outside the area of this diagnostic material.

Fig. 2.1: An approach to diagnostic assessment

in Goodman[8]). This approach clearly enjoys a close affinity with much of the work carried out within profiling.

The two approaches are not mutually exclusive, and work to the best advantage of the pupil when they are used in a complementary manner. The same is true of the third approach which I have suggested – namely the identification of individuals' strengths and interests, which calls for encouragement and channelling rather than remedial action. This can also be linked with self-assessment.

The heuristic approach (involving a qualitative, self-discovery method of assessment) is probably the most useful when identifying strengths. An interesting alternative approach to the identification of interests can be found in the Job Ideas and Information Generator – Computer Assisted Learning (JIIG – CAL) programme, where a complex battery of questions is answered by the student, fed through a computer and emerges with an 'interest profile' revealing the extent of students' interests in each of six categories. This profile is used as the basis for a further series of questions, which finally produces a list of suggested careers compatible with the identified interest areas. These then form the basis for guidance, and further investigation (see Fig. 2.2).

The diagnostic process in JIIG – CAL[9] is a complex operation which it would be impractical to implement within every school activity, but the principle is clear: in all of these approaches to diagnostic assessment the main thrust is to help the student to a higher level of attainment, or a more satisfying utilisation of his or her talents and interests.

An interesting incidental outcome of diagnostic assessment can be the evaluation of the teaching programme, resulting on occasion in the recognition that it is the teacher who may require 'remedial' action! An example of this can be seen in the case of a fifteen year old who, on receiving an 'A' for achievement and a 'C' for effort, was affronted by the comment 'must work harder'. The parents' legitimate response was 'Why? If he's achieving an "A" with little effort, the school is obviously not setting him sufficiently demanding work.'

Profiles are an ideal vehicle both for recording the results of existing, formal, analytical diagnostic tests, and for recording and *encouraging* greater awareness of the more informal diagnosis. One of the central characteristics of effective profiling is the requirement for regular planned review, discussion and recording. This inevitably includes diagnosis within the profiling process. Participation in formative profiling would be meaningless if the teacher was not, as a result, able to identify areas of weakness, to discuss and plan prospective remedial strategies, to monitor progress and, equally important, to identify and encourage strengths.

The place of parents within the field of diagnostic assessment is frequently overlooked. Margaret Reid's report highlights the fact that parents as well as students expressed a need for 'more detailed comment on their work, and *specific advice on how they could improve*. Without this, initial good intentions might dissipate, simply through lack of direction' (my italics).[10]

It appears clear that if diagnosis forms a regular part of the profiling process,

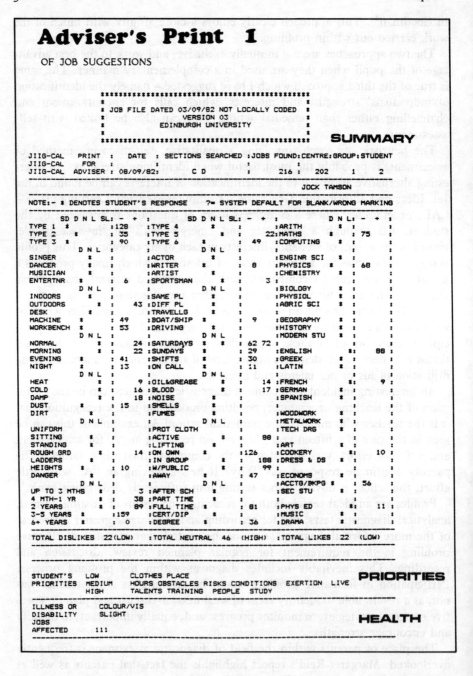

Fig. 2.2: An example from the JIIG – CAL programme

Adviser's Print 2 (Continuation)

```
------------------------------------------------------------------
  9099 CARE ASSISTANT                          PR = 6  CODOT = 443.50

     PRO -
        INTERESTS -    ££TYPE 5
        PEOPLE -       IN GROUP, WITH PUBLIC
        TRAINING -     2 YEARS


  9025 YOUTH & COMMUNITY LEADER                PR = 6  CODOT = 102.16

     PRO -
        INTERESTS -    ££TYPE 5
        TALENTS -      ££SPORTSMAN
        PEOPLE -       WITH PUBLIC
        SUBJECTS -     ENGLISH, PHYSICAL EDUCATION

     CON -                          PROS & CONS
        INTERESTS -    TYPE 6
        TALENTS -      ENTERTAINER
        HOURS -        ££EVENINGS
        TRAINING -     3-5 YEARS
        STUDY -        ££FULL TIME


  9093 POLICEMAN/WOMAN                          PR = 5  CODOT = 411.10

     PRO -
        INTERESTS -    TYPE 5
        CLOTHES -      ££UNIFORM
        PEOPLE -       IN GROUP, WITH PUBLIC
        TRAINING -     ££2 YEARS
        SUBJECTS -     ENGLISH

     CON -
        HOURS -        ££SHIFTS


------------------------------------------------------------------
  SECTIONS SEARCHED        C D
  JOBS PRINTED IN ORDER
                             JOB SUGGESTIONS
  SECTION C
  JOBFILE          JOB TITLE                     PTS   CODOT
  NUMBER                                         RTG

  9099     CARE ASSISTANT                         6   443.50
  3020     NURSERY NURSE                          6   441.25
  3016     NURSE-ENROLLED, SEN/EN                 6   113.34
  3002     AIR STEWARD/STEWARDESS                 6   442.20
  9093     POLICEMAN/WOMAN                        5   411.10
  9067     ARMY- MENS CORPS/W.R.A.C.              5   401.10
  3005     DENTAL SURGERY ASSISTANT               5   443.99
  9063     WAITER/WAITRESS                        5   432.50
  9062     COOK/CHEF                              5   430.10
  3068     DRIVING INSTRUCTOR                     5   099.80


  SECTION D
  JOBFILE          JOB TITLE                     PTS   CODOT
  NUMBER                                         RTG

  9025     YOUTH & COMMUNITY LEADER               6   102.16
  9096     SOCIAL WORKER - RESIDENTIAL            5   102.20
  4003     NURSE-REGISTERED, SRN/RGN             5   113.30
  4029     BEAUTY THERAPIST                       5   471.15
  4027     DENTAL HYGIENIST                       5   119.20
  9078     CHURCH WORKER                          5   109.99
  4015     PHYSIOLOGICAL MEASUREMENT TECHNICIAN   4   119.30
  4011     COURIER/REPRESENTATIVE                 4   442.40
  4028     CARTOGRAPHIC DRAUGHTSMAN               4   253.34
  9094     HOME ECONOMIST                         4   369.10

------------------------------------------------------------------
```

both students and, possibly for the first time, their parents will be given this information.

Both profiles and diagnostic assessment are directly concerned with the personal development of the individual; both use assessment as part of the continuing learning process in order to help the individual to higher levels of attainment.

In this way profiles provide an opportunity to strengthen the area of assessment which is concerned with *helping* the individual, as opposed to the more familiar function of assessment which concerns itself with *judging*.

2.6   Aid staff development (see also 4.5)

The need for massive in-service training allied to the introduction of profiles is often set within a negative context – it is seen as a first-aid activity required to remedy deficiencies in teacher skill, expertise and confidence.

I believe that it is far more helpful to take the in-service provision which must be made available and to use it as a tool which should be identified and exploited in the service of teachers' interests.

This is an opportunity for teachers to benefit from increased in-service education in order to broaden horizons, to keep up to date with new educational developments, to experience interaction with teachers from other institutions and either to acquire or to extend skills in assessment, guidance and counselling.

In a time of economic recession, of contraction and of falling rolls, there are inevitably reduced opportunities for mobility within the profession, and for promotion. Teachers of thirty years of age on a Scale 3 or 4 can face many years without any prospect of promotion. In these circumstances the introduction of profiles can offer new challenges. The associated staff development offers an opportunity to modify and adapt existing routine; it offers the opportunity for cross-fertilisation of ideas and experiences, and the chance to work in collaboration with others, both within the same organisation, and with individuals from other organisations. All of these opportunities can lead to increased job satisfaction, which can help to compensate for the static nature of the profession at the present time.

Resources are limited: the issue of time and resources remains a thorny problem. Nevertheless, the one area in which it appears that some LEAs are prepared to be generous is in the provision of in-service education. It makes sense, even if one is initially sceptical about profiles, to take full advantage of the opportunities available for staff development. Even if profiles finally fall by the wayside, their exploitation as a tool for staff development could prove invaluable.

2.7 Improve selection

The increased level of information recorded and offered to users undoubtedly provides a useful supplement or alternative to existing confidential references. In many cases this wish to provide more information for employers and other users has been a prime consideration for teachers. In the attempt to improve selection, two quite separate, alternative strands are identifiable:

i. The desire of teachers to provide users with a fuller picture of the individual, in the hope that this will help to offset any disadvantage suffered by students unlikely to achieve minimum entry qualifications. It is an understandable and laudable motive; experience of YTS schemes, where major employers such as Marks and Spencer have amended selection procedures, supports this view. Youngsters who would not previously have been considered because they failed to meet examination requirements displayed qualities which made them highly suitable employees. There is, then, evidence that if employers can be made aware of alternative attributes, they might be persuaded to accept those who would previously have been rejected. The same argument can be advanced in the case of profiles, which enable evidence which would otherwise have been unrecorded and unaccredited to be presented and to influence the chances of the young person.

ii. The second motive of those interested in providing fuller information is that of helping employers – to ease the task of selection by using the profile as a finer-meshed screening tool. There is still heavy dependence on the '5 "O" level' type of screening, but there is increasing evidence that employers are now seeking more than mechanistic selectors.

At a recent meeting of a regional CBI/Chamber of Commerce group, employers were asked to list attributes which they considered important in potential employees. The list puts examination results in sixteenth position.

Physical fitness for the job
Manual or finger dexterity
Appropriate appearance, dress, behaviour, clear speech
Neat handwriting
Adequate numeracy, calculating, measurement – (4 rules) arithmetic accuracy
Ability to understand instructions
Capability for training
Capacity to work without supervision
Punctuality and timekeeping
Honesty, trustworthiness and integrity
Willingness to undertake tasks
Responsibility for their materials, tools etc.
Taking initiative
Politeness and courtesy to colleagues and customers

Getting on with people of different age and background
Sat/passed CSE/GCE/'O' and 'A' levels
Capacity to obtain vocational qualification
Capacity to work under stress
Potential for degree or professional exams

Admittedly this is too small a sample from which to extrapolate – one of the greatest difficulties in establishing 'what employers want' lies in the fact that they seem unable to agree common criteria.

The whole question of users' response to profiles is one which requires considerably more research than is currently available, but many major employers have indicated that they would welcome profiles – if not as a replacement for the examination system, at least as a supplement. One training manager of a firm employing 10,000 people was convinced of the potential benefits, not only to employers but to the personal development of young people. He advised 'you will meet resistance from backwoodsmen, but you must be brave and persevere'.

In an ILEA survey of employers views,[11] it was interesting that while the majority sought evidence that students were *taking* 'O' level or CSE courses, the actual result was not a determining factor – in most cases the offer was made well in advance of results. Qualities which were identified as important included getting along with others, showing enthusiasm for the job, good communication skills.

Most employers reacted positively to the ILEA communications profile – one interviewee said: 'This is very impressive, you can't get an awful lot of information from an "O" level.'

Most respondents felt that the profile would be a useful adjunct not an alternative to the examination system. As Henry Mackintosh points out: 'Employers, whilst progressively disenchanted with information they currently receive from examinations and the form in which they receive it, are also ambivalent about changing a system which by and large they understand, for one which could well involve them in more work.'[12]

This highlights the dilemma surrounding the form which any summative profile should take: there are conflicting views from employers regarding whether they are prepared to give due weight to a full, informative document, or whether a brief summary document is all they are prepared to consider.

The HMI report notes that employers who had been directly involved in the development of profiles welcomed them.[13] Most others showed interest but asked for clarification of descriptors such as 'shows initiative'. This particularly highlights two points. First, that if profiles are to achieve recognition, they will require assiduous marketing, both locally and nationally. Second, if profiles are to gain acceptance as complementary to or as an acceptable alternative to public examinations, a great deal of care must be taken in devising instruments which are clear, unambiguous and understandable to a wide range of users.

The schools liaison officer of a major employer has stated that most personnel officers in the company required minimum examination qualifications, but identified areas in which additional information would be useful. These included: personal qualities, ability to work in a team, attitude to work, attendance, punctuality, out of school activities, leadership qualities, practical skills and personal achievements. They particularly valued enthusiasm, determination, co-operation, adaptability, flexibility, and reliability.

These are all qualities which are included in many profiles: it would therefore appear that this employer's conclusion that 'despite caution there is a great deal of evidence of goodwill amongst employers' supports the view that profiles and employers' needs may well prove compatible.

Summary

This chapter has ranged over a broad sweep of issues surrounding the purposes associated with the introduction of profiles. Some of these issues have received widespread attention; others may be less familiar, but are no less significant.

Amongst the more familiar purposes are the arguments demanding the right of every pupil to leave school with a worthwhile leaving certificate – a claim which has been made repeatedly over the last half century, and which, with the Secretary of State's declaration,[14] appears to be nearer realisation than ever before.

Another major issue incorporated in the purposes section is the motivating power of profiles. It is a major concern of many advocating the use of profiles that young people should be helped to gain self-confidence, enhanced self-esteem and greater self-awareness, and to enjoy success emanating from the recognition of positive achievements. It is arguable that such recognition is self-perpetuating, and that young people will become more highly motivated, and, hopefully, will become more self-reliant, autonomous adults.

Allied to this increase in motivation is the role of profiles in placing assessment at the centre of the learning process, where it becomes an aid to diagnosis, of increasing communication as a result of the dialogue which is an integral part of profiling and, as a result, improves relationships between teacher and taught. The whole issue of formative interaction in the assessment process is incorporated in these purposes, together with the implications for a pastoral system which is integrated into the whole curriculum.

The initial purpose of many pioneers was the improvement of existing recording and reporting systems. These are still important functions of profiles, rationalising the often diffuse and disjointed systems currently operating in many schools. There is an arguable role for the use of profiles to enhance teachers' skills and job satisfaction by the increase in in-service education which must inexorably accompany the spread of profiles.

Finally, on a more mechanistic level, the function of profiles as a possible aid to selection by employers, FE and YTS schemes is also discussed.

The amalgam of all of these purposes produces a new, innovative strategy, pointing the way towards curriculum innovation on a large scale. It calls not only for innovation in what is assessed – by implication, we value what we assess. Consequently, what is assessed by the profile, whether it be cross-curricular skills or personal qualities, will demand a higher priority in the allocation of teachers' time and energies. In many cases it means that the hidden curriculum will be made explicit.

This in turn calls for a change in teachers' approach to their teaching – some call it a revolution. It is a revolution which many teachers are embracing with enthusiasm. Others are understandably sceptical, or full of trepidation. It was probably an unintentioned call to revolution in the early days, but it is certainly the case that many protagonists now see the possibility to change entrenched attitudes and practices as one of the aims of profiling. The one unanimous purpose which unites those with many differing views and motives is that profiles should offer a fairer deal to young people: this, after all, is what profiling is all about.

Notes

1. Department of Education and Science, and Welsh Office, *Records of achievement: a statement of policy*, 1984.
2. *Ibid*.
3. Hargreaves, D., *Interpersonal relations and education*, Routledge and Kegan Paul, 1972.
4. *Ibid*.
5. See Hitchcock, Gloria, The Avon Initiative, in Further Education Unit, *Profiles in action*, 1984.
6. Pearce, B., *Review of personal record systems on educational schemes*, Counselling and Career Development Unit, Leeds University, 1979.
7. Satterly, D., *Assessment in schools*, Basil Blackwell, 1981.
8. Goodman, K., Reading: a psycholinguistic guessing game, in Singer H, and Ruddell R. (eds.), *Theoretical models and processes of reading*, Newark Del: International Reading Association, 1970.
9. Closs, S.J., *Job ideas and information generator: computer assisted learning*, Handbook for tutors, University of Edinburgh, 1980.
10. Reid M., School reports to parents: a study of policy and practice in secondary schools, *Educational Research*, Vol. 26, June 1984.
11. Varlam, C., *Exploratory study of employers' views on the ILEA/RSA profiling scheme*, unpublished paper, 1982.
12. Mackintosh, H., The prospects for public examinations in England and Wales, *Educational Analysis* **4**, 3, pp. 13–20, 1982.
13. HMI *Records of achievement at 16+: some examples of current practice*, HMSO, 1983.
14. Department of Education and Science, and Welsh Office, *Records of achievement*.

Chapter 3

Main categories of profiles

This chapter looks at main approaches to the recording of profile assessments. It offers a summary of the characteristics of each, the advantages and disadvantages, the position of each type on the formative → summative line, and some examples in practice, together with participants' views. These views do not represent a full-scale independent evaluation – there is a dearth of such evaluative evidence – but give a flavour of practitioners' responses.

The main categories, and individual examples of profiles, can be placed within a framework spanning the line between formative and summative. The sample of profiles examined has been divided into five baseline categories:

3.1 Student recording:
    A. of personal achievements, experiences and interests, e.g. RPA, PPR;
    B. of self-assessments, involving a more critical analysis of strengths and weaknesses leading to greater self-awareness, e.g. Can-do cards.

3.2 Student–teacher negotiated records: where both student and teacher participate in negotiating comments recorded on the profile, e.g. Comberton Village College, Avon Student Profile.

3.3 Criterion checklists: where student achievement is matched against a list of predetermined criteria, e.g. Evesham High School, RSA.

3.4 Comment banks: where appropriate comments can be selected from a prepared bank, and formulated to produce an individual prose statement relating to the student, e.g. Clwyd profile, Welsh profile.

3.5 Grid-style profiles: where a series of hierarchical statements (usually between four and six) can be ticked to indicate the level of student achievement, e.g. SCRE, City and Guilds (see Fig. 3.1).

3.1A Student recording of personal achievements (see also 7.10)

Student recording can be placed very firmly at the formative end of the spectrum. It is not, strictly speaking, profiling, because it consists entirely of the student's record of personal achievements, experiences and interests with no comment or assessment by teachers. However, it is included because it has been very influential in developing the formative aspects of profiling.

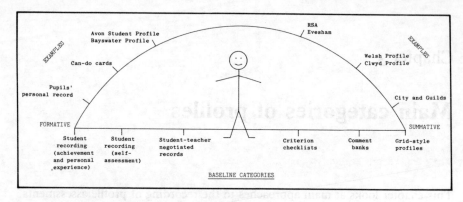

Fig. 3.1: Main categories of profiles

a. Record of Personal Achievement (RPA)

Don Stansbury was instrumental in developing first RPA in the early 70s,[1] and later Record of Personal Experience under the 'Diamond Challenge programme' which is sponsored by the Springline Trust.[2]

An essential feature of both schemes, which are very similar, is that the record is the student's property, and that the recording which takes place is chosen by the pupil – there is no teacher direction, censorship or assessment. The aim is to provide a rewarding and revealing formative activity which can help young people to understand themselves better.

Recording takes place on loose leaf cards, which are fitted into an impressive folder as they are completed (see Fig. 3.2). An independent evaluation of RPA found that there was evidence to support claims that RPA provides a framework for incentive and motivation, particularly for those for whom examinations are not appropriate, but that it does not act successfully as a leaving qualification.[3]

b. Pupil Personal Recording (PPR)

This is a development which emerged from the work on RPA and which is similar in many respects. PPR claims to be different in that it should:
  i. be available to all pupils of all abilities
 ii. complement existing examinations
iii. develop close involvement of parents and teachers.

Once again the emphasis is on formative recording, and confidentiality is extended to the point where teachers may not see students' work without permission (students' permission was required in order to use the illustrations in this book).

One of the principal aims is to improve the students' self-image: an important part of this, in common with other forms of profiling, is to encourage young people to recognise that many of the activities which they undertake, and to which they attach little value, are in fact worth recognising.

WORK EXPERIENCE

JOB Serving chips

PLACE John's fish and Chips shop.

WORK CARRIED OUT I have got a little job in a fish and chip shop.
I work Tuesday, Wednesday, Thursday and Fridays.
On a Tuesday night I work 6·30 until 11·o'clock. On Wednesday,
Thursday and Friday I work 6·30 until 8·30.
I get £1·00 an hour. I like it up there because I meet
nice people. When I work on Tuesday nights we get
drunks in the shop, but I live near the shop so I know
most of them. I like it very much and when I leave
school if I can get a job in the daytime I will. I will
never leave the shop. If I cant get a job I will
be able to work up there day and night.

SIGNED S.J. Cunningham.   POSITION   DATE 26·4·80.

Fig. 3.2: Record of Personal Achievement

ACTIVITY Ice Skating

DATE	DESCRIPTION	SIGNED	POSITION
11·2·88	Ice skating		
	In my ghass m° P.P.R we		
	went Ice skating with		
	the Teacher, some went		
	By car, and some went		
	By mini Bus, do we got		
	aut of the Bus it was		
	snoeing, we went in° the		
	Ice skating place, miss		
	asked me if I would do		
	Ice skating I said no, I will		
	Just watch, mr cooper asked me		
	to take some pictures off the glass		
	Debra Fell down on the Ace, And		
	hinda would'nt go round on the ice		

NAME Inoanie

Fig. 3.3: Pupil's Personal Record

One youngster from a very deprived background was amazed to realise that the boring chores of putting the younger children to bed at night, and doing the shopping, could be considered worthwhile activities, making a real contribution to the welfare of the family.

Recording can even help young people to come to terms with more serious problems – a girl in one school took the 'Away from home' section literally, and wrote twenty-two cards about being taken into care. It helped her over a bad patch, and she said 'I feel better now'.

It is significant that findings from a pilot programme of PPR carried out in eight LEAs in the West Country reveal that whilst the formative function of PPR is very effective, hopes that it would extend to more able students have not, in the main, been fulfilled (see Fig. 3.3).

c. Record of Personal Experience (RPE)

Stansbury, one of the originators of RPA, helped to set up the Springline Trust in order to promote the personal recording of experience for students. According to the Trust, seven principles should govern the activity:

   i. The process is more important than the product.
  ii. A personal record is made by the person concerned.
 iii. The purpose of a personal record is to communicate.
  iv. The recorder controls the reading of the record.
   v. Personal records are records of experience rather than records of achievement.
  vi. Nothing that appears in a personal record should be thought by a reader to be trivial.
 vii. A record of personal experience is a distillation. It cannot be further distilled by someone else.

In this latest project, based on earlier experience, the value of the *process* as a formative tool is strongly emphasised.

d. Student recording as part of a profile

As thinking about profiles has developed, more and more schools are realising the importance of student recording, and are including at least a small section within the profile (see Fig. 3.4).

This may vary from a section in which the student records throughout the year, to a single sheet which the whole class completes at one sitting (which has less formative value than open recording).

e. One school's approach to student recording

A girls' comprehensive (Pen Park School) with experience of RPA adopted PPR and took part in the piloting process. In practice, it is usually the lower achieving students who opt for PPR, although increasingly students are studying for one or two examinations in addition to PPR.

In this particular school one tutor assumes responsibility for the group (the pattern varies in other schools). This enables a close relationship to be formed

HELSTON SCHOOL PROFILE

Name_____ Tutor Group_____

INTERESTS and ACHIEVEMENTS

Pupils should complete this section with details and
comment upon their outside and school interests,
achievements, part-time work, hobbies, etc.

PUPIL'S SIGNATURE _____ DATE _____

Fig. 3.4

between pupil and teacher. It also facilitates group activities such as regular excursions which help to broaden horizons, and also give the young people material for entry into their folders.

It is axiomatic that students are not directed to record at set times – it is their own choice. Whilst the tutor respects the right to privacy, in practice the work is usually freely discussed, and some illuminating insights can be obtained.

f. What participants feel about student recording

The PPR tutor saw the value of recording as being entirely weighted towards self-development of the individual: 'The formative part is vital – I don't think PPR has any place as a summative document.' It is interesting, however, that she did see the possibility of building on this part: 'I think that student recording as an element of profiling, working towards a final profile, would be very possible.' Views of other staff varied, but most saw it as a useful motivator, though without the status enjoyed by examinations.

The work experience organiser found that co-operation with the PPR tutor '. . . makes the pupils realise that their work experience is valuable, helps them to focus on what they have learnt and experienced, and links their work in school with their experience in the outside world'.

Most of the young people participating in the scheme enjoyed it. One girl from the lowest ability band remarked, with great perception: 'I like PPR because the limelight is on you, and not on the teacher.' The same girl gained superb reports from her work experience; she later gained work as an apprentice hairdresser, but when told that it was well deserved, said: '. . . but I failed at school. All my CSEs were ungraded', which sadly illuminates the negative effects of examinations on young people, in contrast to the positive self-image which student recording tries to foster.

Evidence of the pride which students took in their PPR folders could be found in their requests to teachers to sign and authenticate their entries. On one occasion there was a detectable air of excitement as they waited for the teacher to sign their cards – not the usual response to marking of homework!

Completed documents have traditionally been presented at a ceremony, either as part of Speech Day, or in a separate ceremony. On the whole these occasions have been well supported; the students appear proud to receive their folders. On one moving occasion when a pupil could not attend, her mother took her place, receiving the folder on her daughter's behalf.

g. Advantages of student recording

   i. The formative learning process is given a very high priority. Students' self-development is recognised as being crucial to the whole activity.
   ii. Personal recording can help to enhance students' self-esteem, self-confidence and feelings of personal worth.
   iii. The process, with increased personal contact, conversations and outside visits, helps to improve communication between student and teacher.
   iv. Improved communication can, in itself, lead to better relationships.

v. Improved self-knowledge can lead the student towards self-assessment – the type of assessment which will matter most in adult life (see 3.1B).
vi. The impressive dossier can offer prospective employers a fund of revealing information.
vii. Student recording used as part of a profile offers young people a chance to reveal their own interests, achievements and qualities.
viii. This also offers a more complete, rounded picture to any user.

h. Disadvantages of student recording
i. There is no summative element.
ii. As a result of this, personal records have a low currency value in terms of gaining entry to employment or FE.
iii. There is a danger that recording is engaged in principally by the lower ability pupils, exacerbating a 'sheep and goats' situation.
iv. This engenders the further hazard of lowering the value of the activity and of the record in the eyes of the pupils themselves, their peers and their teachers.
v. If student recording is adopted for *all* students, it could require a great deal of time.

i. Summary for potential users of student recording
A very clear message comes across in this section: student recording is uncompromisingly *formative*.

If you want a process which concentrates on self-development, motivation and all the other characteristics of a formative process (see Chapters 2 and 4) then student recording is for you.

If, however, your organisation seeks to produce something with an end report, a summative certificate, then personal recording as described in the examples in this chapter will not fit the bill.

This should not, however, exclude you from considering the part that a more modest attempt at recording can play in the whole process of profiling. This section has shown that there are valuable lessons to be learned from allowing young people to participate in their own recording, reporting and assessment, rather than expecting them to accept the process as something which is 'done to them by teachers'.

3.1B   Student recording of self-assessments

Perhaps the most relevant form of assessment in terms of preparing for adult life is self-assessment. This approach has long been used in careers education, where young people have been asked to assess themselves over a range of qualities and abilities, but self-assessment can usefully be extended across the whole range of learning and experience within schools (see Fig. 3.5).

It is regarded with suspicion by some, who feel that students' self-assessment

WHO AM I ?			SECTION 1 (Social Skills)

Tick the column you think is most like you.

Do this on your <u>own</u> or if you prefer with your group.

	Very much like me	Like me sometimes	Not at all like me
<u>Meeting and greeting people</u>			
I always find it easy to meet and greet my friends.	✓		
I am embarrassed when I meet people of my own age whom I do not know very well.		✓	
I enjoy meeting adults.			✓
<u>Putting people at their ease</u>			
I am good with shy people.		✓	
I hang back when someone new arrives.			✓
I can always help someone who does not know what to do next.	✓		
I am no good with a younger child who is crying.			✓
<u>Listening</u>			
I can always help someone who has difficulty in explaining something.		✓	
I am embarrassed by other people's troubles.			✓
I know how to encourage a shy person to talk more freely.		✓	
I can keep quiet when it is necessary.	✓		
<u>Coping with difficult situations</u>			
I lose my temper when people are difficult.		✓	
I can usually help people settle their differences when they are quarrelling.		✓	
I know how to help someone who is being teased or insulted.	✓		

I feel that I would like to become better at:-

1) Meeting adults

2) Not losing my temper when people are difficult

3)

Fig. 3.5a: Self-assessment form from Hartcliffe School

SELF-ASSESSMENT IN ENGLISH

Think about your work in English

1.   Which things have you enjoyed doing?

2.   Which things do you think you have done well?

3.   Are there any things you have avoided doing?

4.   Where do you need help and advice?

Tick below

- ☐ Reading
- ☐ Writing stories
- ☐ Writing poems
- ☐ Handwriting
- ☐ Spelling
- ☐ Full-stops
- ☐ Speechmarks
- ☐ 's
- ☐ How to take notes
- ☐ Interviewing or discussion
- ☐ Drama
- ☐ Finding things in the library
- ☐ In something not listed here. If so write it here.

Which of these do you think you should improve first?

5.   How do you think you can improve your work?

6.   Write a short <u>report</u> on your work in English. Tell the truth about yourself.

Fig. 3.5b

Can you add, subtract, divide and multiply whole numbers using pen and paper

For example

$$237 + 321 = \qquad 70 - 14 =$$

$$141 \times 7 = \qquad 348 \div 4 =$$

Can you use a calculator or adding machine

Can you add, subtract, divide and multiply fractions using pen and paper

For example

$$\tfrac{1}{4} + {}^{13}/_{16} = \qquad 2\tfrac{3}{4} \times \tfrac{1}{4} =$$

$$1\tfrac{1}{2} - \tfrac{3}{8} = \qquad 99 \div 3\tfrac{1}{3} =$$

Can you measure distance using a rule or tape measure to the nearest millimetre or sixteenth of an inch

---

Can you add, subtract, divide and multiply decimals using pen and paper

For example

$$\begin{array}{r} 1.73\ + \\ 3.70 \\ \hline \end{array} \qquad \begin{array}{r} 3.78\ - \\ 1.40 \\ \hline \end{array}$$

$$3.5 \times 7.8 = \qquad 18.6 \div 1.2 =$$

Can you use a pair of scales or a balance to measure weight in pounds and ounces and in kilogrammes and grammes

---

Can you carry out simple mental arithmetic

For example

Subtract 35p from £1.00

Add 50 cm to 1 metre 75 cm

Can you measure liquids in jugs or cans in pints (imperial) and litres (metric)

Fig. 3.6: Examples of 'Can-do' cards

Instructions

Enter those skills and needs which the young person has identified in the appropriate column below, using the number shown on the card.

If several skills or needs are identified which have equal importance, write the numbers alongside each other eg 2, 7, 11 etc.

Order	Pile 1 (Skills possessed) Card Number	Order	Pile 2 (Skills where help is needed) Card Number
1 2 3 4 5 6 7 8 9 10 11 12 13 14 15 16 17 18 19 20 21		1 2 3 4 5 6 7 8 9 10 11 12 13 14 15 16 17 18 19 20 21	

Additional Strengths

. . . .

. . . .

Additional Needs

. . . .

. . . .

Name:

Signed: Date:

Fig. 3.7: Recording sheet for the 'Can-do' cards

will inevitably err on the side of being unrealistically high. In fact, young people are surprisingly honest – discrepancies more often occur from adopting too low an assessment.

a. Can-do cards and profiles
One attempt to incorporate significant self-assessment can be found in the 'Can-do' cards developed by Freshwater and Oates.[4] Originally devised for a training workshop situation, they can be adapted for a wide range of purposes.

Intended both as an aid to identifying an individual's strengths and weakness, and as a means of establishing areas requiring further help, it is designed as a card game.

  i. A number of cards – see examples – are considered by trainee and administrator;
 ii. they are then placed into two piles according to whether the trainee feels that he or she possesses the skills or not;
iii. cards in each pile are then placed in rank order according to relative strength or weakness;
 iv. the cards are numbered and these numbers can then be transferred to the profile (see Figs. 3.6 and 3.7) for easy interpretation.

b. The Village College, Comberton
The Comberton Record of Achievement profile is an example of a school paying more than lip-service to the concept of self-assessment. The profile produces statements about students with regard to:
  i. interest and leisure activities
 ii. work experience
iii. personal qualities
 iv. academic performance
  v. work skills
 vi. future prospects.

One of the stated principles is that the profile should '. . . have a large element of pupil self-assessment'. Student self-assessments are made in the 3rd, 4th and 5th years by the *student* (see Fig. 3.8). The way in which these are incorporated into a final statement of achievement is discussed on page 54 (an example of the way in which the boundaries of profiles may blur and spread across several approaches to recording), but it is clear that in this scheme, self-assessment is viewed as being equally as important as teacher assessment.

c. What participants feel about self-assessment
One teacher who had attempted some self-assessment with his students said: 'It was a complete washout – they lied from start to finish!'. This was a minority view, however (and one could ask questions about the perspective adopted by this teacher); others disagreed, and found their students honest to a fault. Most teachers found that students are interested and involved when engaged upon self-assessment exercises – after all, what is more absorbing than a contemplation of oneself!

One youth, who had been extremely introverted, was able to recognise this, to build on it through the year, and at the end not only assess himself as having increased his ability to communicate with others, but to point to evidence illustrating this specific quality. He was equally willing to point out a lack of energy and enthusiasm in another field, which he attributed to a lack of interest.

Most young people appeared to appreciate the opportunity to have their own view of themselves given serious consideration.

d. Advantages of student self-assessment
i. Self-assessment can promote a greater sense of student involvement.
ii. This can, in itself, improve communication and understanding between teacher and student.
iii. Motivation can be enhanced.
iv. The student's self-assessment can provide valuable information for the teacher, about both the individual, and the effectiveness of the course.
v. Self-assessment can help in the diagnosis of strengths and weaknesses and, as a consequence, help the individual to progress to higher levels of attainment.

e. Disadvantages of student self-assessment
i. Self-assessment may not be particularly beneficial if it is carried out only once – it would appear to be more beneficial if it is part of a rolling programme.
ii. There may be difficulties in accepting the evidence of self-assessment as being objective.
iii. Individualised self-assessment can be time-consuming.
iv. It may not be considered sufficient for a summative report.
v. Students need to learn the skills of self-assessment.

f. Summary for potential users of self-assessment
It is clear that a very useful tool in terms of the development of self-awareness, enhanced self-image and increased confidence and motivation can be found in the use of student self-assessment. The emphasis is unquestionably formative, and it may be felt necessary to incorporate it into a hybrid approach in order to gain a balanced picture. However, there is nothing inherent in student self-assessment which makes it unsuitable for inclusion within any particular technique, and if you are engaged in developing profiles within your institution, you may find this a useful source of inspiration.

3.2   Student–teacher negotiated records (see also 7.8)

Strictly speaking, this is not a type of profile, but a tenet of profiling which can run through every form of recording assessment. However, it is such an

Cambridgeshire   Chief Education Officer
                                            G. H. Morris B.A.

Record of Achievement

Warden:
K. FOREMAN, B.A., M.ED.   THE VILLAGE COLLEGE,

                                             COMBERTON,

                                             CAMBRIDGE CB3 7DU

                                             COMBERTON (022 026) 2503

Name .... Tutor Group ....

Address ....

Date of Birth ....

Date of entry to the College .... Leaving date ....

VALIDATED AND ACCREDITED BY THE GOVERNING
BODY OF THE VILLAGE COLLEGE, COMBERTON

This document contains the following sections :

1) Interest and Leisure Activities   2) Work Experience
3) Personal Qualities   4) Work Skills
5) Future Prospects   6) Subjects Studied

This document is a summary.
Further information is available from the college.

Fig. 3.8: The Comberton Record of Achievement Profile

1)   <u>Interest and Leisure Activities</u>
        <u>Student's Statement</u>

        <u>Statement by the College</u>

---

2)   <u>Work Experience</u>
        <u>Student's Statement</u>

        <u>Statement by the College</u>

---

3)   <u>Personal Qualities</u>
        <u>Student's Statement</u>

        <u>Statement by the College</u>

---

4)   <u>Work Skills</u>
        <u>Student's Statement</u>

        <u>Statement by the College</u>

---

5)   <u>Future Prospects</u>
        <u>Student's Statement</u>

        <u>Statement by the College</u>

---

6)   <u>Subjects Studied</u>

Subject	Type of Exam G.C.E./C.S.E./R.S.A.	Expected Grade	Actual Result

Student's signature   College Statement Compiled by

....

Date.........................

NOTE: Larger spaces allowed in original

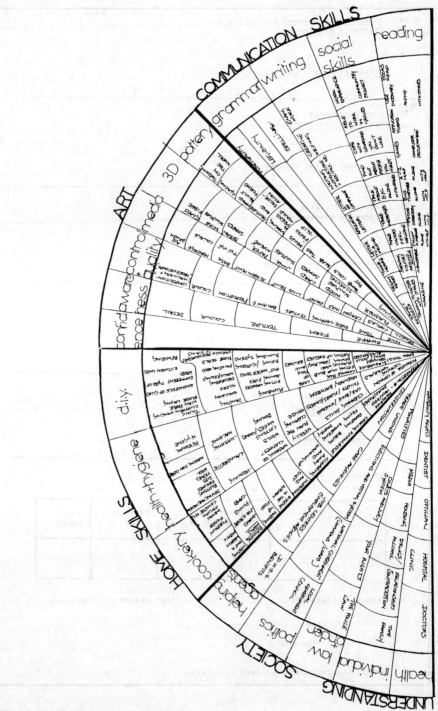

Fig. 3.9: The Bayswater Profile

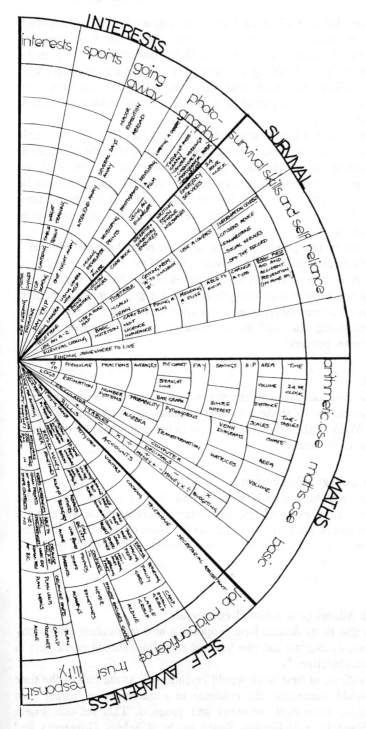

important concept that it is allocated a separate category here. This approach to profiling is really quite revolutionary; the term 'negotiation' was catapulted to the forefront of educational terminology with the publication of *A basis for choice*.[5] The concept of negotiating assessment or curriculum objectives with students was one which, whilst meeting with some resistance, has since been adopted in many FE courses – particularly those concerned with vocational or pre-vocational education.

For obvious reasons, the idea of negotiating, or even involving young people in their own assessment, has taken a great deal longer to percolate into schools (with certain honourable exceptions). However, there are a number of initiatives which seek to implement this approach – most of which, it must be conceded, are in the early stages of development. Where it has been introduced, teachers have become aware of the benefits which can accrue from student participation.

The edges between the previous section and the next three are blurred – there is inevitably an element of self-assessment in student–teacher negotiation.

An unnecessary degree of anxiety is sometimes caused by the word 'negotiation' – this does not mean that 'everything is up for grabs' as some teachers have put it – there are, inevitably, constraints upon what is open to negotiation. It *does* mean including the students in setting learning objectives and in discussing their own progress.

a. Can-do cards

This system has been described in the previous section – the self-assessment element leads inevitably to student–teacher negotiation in identifying future learning needs. Many of the YTS schemes now in operation adopt a negotiated approach to profile assessment.

b. The Village College, Comberton

Again, self-assessment links closely with student–teacher negotiation. In this instance students' self-assessments are sent home to parents in the 4th and 5th year alongside teachers' statements, and form the basis of formative dialogue. The final 'statement of achievement' is the culmination of this dialogue, and is an example of the practical possibilities of engaging in a very real form of student–teacher negotiation.

c. Burgess and Adams (a negotiated curriculum)

Tyrrell Burgess and Betty Adams have proposed a new curriculum philosophy whereby students, during the last two years of schooling, should participate in setting their own objectives.[6]

A folder of evidence of best work would be collected; at the end of the time each student would summarise the evidence in a statement of his/her own skills, competence, attainment, interests and progress. This self-assessment would be validated by a Validation Board made of School Governors and others, and externally accredited by an Accreditation Board made up of professionals, including inspectors and teachers from other schools, which would reassure students, teachers and users that the records could be depended upon.

This proposed approach, whilst not yet in operation, is adding a new dimension to the debate on the negotiated curriculum.

d. The Bayswater Profile

The Bayswater Centre, Bristol, enjoys considerable success in offering a more relevant curriculum to youngsters who have rejected school.

The profile (see Fig. 3.9) has been developed as a motivating tool, and provides a basis for negotiating a learning programme and for negotiated assessment. The aim is undeniably formative.

This profile is included not because it is influential nationally, but as an illustration of the ingenuity which a small institution has brought to bear in developing an approach to assessment which is designed to encourage realistic self-assessment, a negotiated curriculum and a genuinely formative interaction between student and teacher.

e. The Avon Student Profile

In an attempt to capitalise on existing work, the County of Avon Working Party on Profiles developed a draft which it hoped would meet the need for a formative profiling process leading to a final summative statement.

The profile, which will undergo modification during the piloting process, consists of four sections:

  i. personal achievements
  ii. personal qualities
 iii. basic skills
  iv. school subject attainment.

All four sections are designed to help students learn about themselves and their education and it is envisaged that all sections would be discussed with teachers.

Two of the sections in particular – personal qualities and school subject attainment – are designed to encourage student–teacher negotiation.

Personal qualities (see also 6.2a and 7.5)
In an attempt to avoid the dangers inherent in teachers passing judgement on the personal qualities of their students, the young people would be asked to assess themselves on qualities which *they* select. The form would then be passed to the tutor for discussion and comment (see Figs. 3.10 and 3.11).

School subject attainment (see also 6.2d and 7.5)
At the beginning of each half term the pupil, under the guidance of the teacher, will set out immediate objectives in the specified subject. At the end of the half term the pupil will comment on his or her attainment in the light of these objectives (see Fig. 3.12).

It is, as yet, too early to estimate the impact of this process on pupils and

Self Reliance, Resourcefulness, Independence

> How much am I able to do things for myself without expecting others to show me or help me?

Initiative, Leadership

> How willing am I to take the lead or think of things to do?

Responsibility, Reliability

> How much do I take on something to do, and do it as well as I can without being checked up on?

Perseverance, Determination

> How much do I stick at something even if it is difficult?

Carefulness

> How much am I able to do something carefully and well rather than in a hurry and badly?

Originality, Creativeness

> How much do I think of things for myself and not copy other people?

Adaptability, Flexibility

> How good am I at changing my mind or my attitude when things around me change?

Energy and Enthusiasm

> How much energy and enthusiasm do I show when I take on something to do?

Relationships with authority, parents, adults and own age group

> How do I get on with other people in different circumstances?

Co-operation

> How willing am I to work with other people and to fit in with them?

Awareness of others

> How much am I able to listen to, understand and sympathise with other people and their needs?

Appearance

> What do I look like to other people in the way I dress and keep myself clean?

Fig. 3.10: Personal qualities (Avon Student Profile)

```
NAME OF STUDENT: .........................     Tutor Group ......
                                               Date sheet
                                               completed ........
```

Quality

Student's Comment		Tutor's Comment

Quality

Student's Comment		Tutor's Comment

Quality

Student's Comment		Tutor's Comment

Fig. 3.11: Personal qualities assessment sheet (Avon Student Profile)

```
                    SCHOOL SUBJECT ASSESSMENT


STUDENT'S NAME:    ....................     GROUP/SET..............
                                SUBJECT:..............
TUTOR'S NAME:     .....................     LEVEL OF
                                            GROUP/SET ..............
TUTOR GROUP: ........................
                                            NAME OF TEACHER
                                            OF GROUP/SET ...........
```

STUDENT ASSESSMENT	SUBJECT OBJECTIVES	SUBJECT TEACHER'S ASSESSMENT	TUTOR'S INITIALS

Fig. 3.12: School subject attainment (Avon Student Profile)

teachers, but it offers a way of making the formative aspects of profiling a central part of the school curriculum and the school assessment policy.

f. Advantages of a student–teacher negotiated profile
   i. It increases communication between student and teacher.
  ii. In consequence, improved relationships are facilitated.
 iii. Involvement in setting learning objectives increases student motivation.
  iv. Feedback from students can improve teachers' awareness of the effectiveness of their teaching.
   v. Granting increased initiative and responsibility for their own assessment enhances students' self-confidence and improves attainment.
  vi. Involving students in the process of negotiation enables them to be made aware of the purpose of their own assessment; the learning process is given far more relevance.
 vii. Participation, as opposed to passivity, is surely the most effective route to learning.

g. Disadvantages of a student–teacher negotiated profile
   i. Individualised, or even group, student–teacher negotiation is inevitably more time-consuming than a formal 'chalk and talk' approach.
  ii. Conflict of personalities may cause problems.
 iii. The staff development required in order to prepare teachers in terms of counselling and assessment skills will involve increased resources.

h. Summary for potential users of student–teacher negotiation
Talk to students about the curriculum? Let them negotiate some of their own
programme? Allow them a say in their own assessment?

Unthinkable heresy to some. Yet more and more teachers are seeing this as
an exciting opportunity to establish new relationships within school, to motivate the growing army of disaffected youngsters no longer inspired by the
carrot of examinations which do not lead to jobs, and to take a fresh look at
a curriculum too long dominated by the straightjacket of examinations.

It is obvious that this section has concerned itself almost exclusively with
the formative function of negotiated curriculum and assessment, yet there is
a greater opportunity for including the outcome in a summative report than in
previous approaches.

If you are seeking a profiling technique which will involve minimum disruption to the status quo, and which may be superimposed upon the existing
system, then this approach will not serve your purpose.

If, however, you are seeking to reappraise the curriculum and reporting
system, to develop a curriculum which will have more relevance to a greater
number of students, and which will offer the opportunity for a truly formative
profiling process, then the negotiated student–teacher record deserves your
serious consideration.

3.3 Criterion checklists (see also 7.10)

This involves a checklist of skills, which may be validated when the student
masters an agreed level of performance in each skill, for example: 'read a short
article, letter or detailed notice in clear handwritten form' or 'locate information in a library or filing system'.[7]

The result of this approach is that in a class of thirty students all may gain
credit for a particular skill, or only one or two students may gain credit – the
emphasis is on recognising achievement at a specified level, and not on grading
or sorting.

Criterion checklists try, as far as possible, to remove the element of subjectivity involved in assessment – RSA in particular is chary of commenting on
personal qualities.

a. The Evesham Profile
One of the most influential school-based developments in the field of profiles
has been that pioneered by Evesham High School, which is a mixed comprehensive with approximately 950 pupils.

In 1973, staff in the school, anxious to provide their students with a school-
leaving certificate, produced a grid-style 'inclines to x, inclines to y' type of
record. It was soon abandoned as teachers found it a negative document,
particularly for the low achievers, and students did not value it.

After much discussion both within the school, and with employers, a new
document was devised in 1978/9 designed to give credit for achievement, and

LANGUAGE SKILLS

	Staff	Date	Stamp
1. Has legible handwriting			
2. Can write in sentences			
3. Can read and understand a popular newspaper			
4. Can follow a set of spoken instructions			
5. Reads with fluency and expression			
6. Can use basic punctuation correctly			
7. Avoids elementary spelling mistakes			
8. Speaks clearly and with confidence			
9. Can write a personal letter			
10. Can give and take a telephone message			
11. Can accurately complete a driving licence application			
12. Can write a business letter			
13. Can use the library Dewey classification system			
14. Can extract information from reference books			
15. Can make an accurate written report			
16. Can make a clear spoken public report			
17. Can summarise accurately a notice or report			
18. Can write a personal letter in a foreign language			
19. Can understand simple instructions in a foreign language			
20. Can give simple instructions in a foreign language			

PRACTICAL SKILLS

	Staff	Date	Stamp
1. Is aware of safety precautions in the home			
2. Can use correctly a domestic washing machine			
3. Can iron correctly a shirt or a dress			
4. Can use correctly a domestic sewing machine			
5. Is competent in basic cookery skills			
6. Is able to plan, organise and prepare a family meal			
7. Has an understanding of the importance of a balanced diet			
8. Can understand a working drawing or pattern			
9. Is aware of safety precautions in the workshop			
10. Can use appropriate hand tools correctly			
11. Works carefully and achieves an acceptable standard of finish			
12. Is competent in basic woodwork/metalwork techniques			
13. Can make 3 simple joints in wood or metal			
14. Is competent in basic machine work			
15. Has produced a good/excellent piece of practical work			
16. Understands technical terms in common use			
17. Can express ideas in sketch or diagram form			
18. Has some appreciation of aesthetic values			
19. Can type accurately at 20 w.p.m.			
20. Has shown responsibility in the care of a young child for a short period of time			

Fig. 3.13: Extracts from the Evesham Profile

PERSONAL AND SOCIAL SKILLS

	Staff	Date	Stamp
1. Is normally and cleanly dressed for school			
2. Is normally punctual			
3. Has a good attendance record			
4. Is courteous and well mannered			
5. Is reliable and helpful in school			
6. Is willing to accept advice			
7. Is self-confident in normal school situations			
8. Has consistently made an effort with school work			
9. Takes a pride in his/her work			
10. Can work well without close supervision			
11. Can work well as a member of a group			
12. Can organise his./her work efficiently			
13. Has played for a school team			
14. Can swim 25 metres			
15. Is a regular member of a school club or society			
16. Has attended a school residential course or expedition			
17. Has helped at school functions			
18. Has taken part in school or year assemblies			
19. Has had a position of responsibility at school			
20. Shows a capacity for organisation and leadership			

MATHS SKILLS

	Staff	Date	Stamp
1. Has good accuracy in handling numbers			
2. Capable of performing everyday calculations in money accurately			
3. Able to understand everyday decimals including degrees of accuracy			
4. Able to handle fractions met in everyday life			
5. Is able to work with 12 hour and 24 hour clock systems			
6. Understands money transactions such as wages and income tax			
7. Can convert British currency to the major foreign currencies			
8. Understands simple percentages			
9. Understands metric system of measure			
10. Understands English measures of length, weight and capacity			
11. Can interpret graphical information			
12. Is able to use a calculator			
13. Able to give a rough numerical estimate			
14. Has an understanding of V.A.T.			
15. Understands simple profit and loss			
16. Can read and understand time tables, wage tables and ready reckoner			
17. Has an understanding of banking procedures			
18. Understands area and perimeter of square, rectangle, triangle and circle			
19. Understands area/volume of cuboid, cylinder and prism			
20. Understands averages and can calculate averages from various types of data			

Mathematics and Science Skills	Staff Signature						
1. Can add and subtract whole numbers.							
2. Can add and subtract decimals.							
3. Can multiply and divide whole numbers.							
4. Can multiply and divide decimals.							
5. Can use fractions.							
6. Can understand and use percentages.							
7. Can understand and use the metric system.							
8. Can understand tabular information and graphs.							
9. Can perform speed and time calculations.							
10. Can handle simple equations and formulae.							
11. Can use a calculator to perform basic operations.							
12. Can take readings accurately.							
13. Can use apparatus correctly, safely and work methodically.							
14. Observes carefully and records observations neatly.							
15. Can write simple account of experiments carried out.							
16. Can draw conclusions from experimental results.							
17. Can devise simple experiments to test own ideas.							
18. Can understand basic scientific principles.							
19. Can formulate and apply general principles to commonplace and familiar problems.							
20. Can assess accuracy of results and appreciate source of errors.							

Practical and Creative Skills							
1. Has reached an acceptable standard.							
2. Has a good understanding of theory.							
3. Can put theory into practice.							
4. Can work carefully and has a good standard of finish.							
5. Has good coordination of hand and eye.							
6. Is able to evaluate a problem and take steps to solve it.							
7. Can use machinery and tools competently and according to safety regulations.							
8. Can make accurate technical drawings.							
9. Shows a good understanding of the principles of design.							
10. Understands basic elements of agriculture.							
11. Is helpful and cooperative in carrying out the more repetitive jobs in cookery.							
12. Is able to plan, organise and prepare a family meal.							
13. Is observant and can draw and paint competently.							
14. Can plan and work competently in Pottery/Weaving.							
15. Has artistic ability.							
16. Is able to manipulate a typewriter and use all the mechanisms fully.							
17. Is able to apply the above skills in the writing of straightforward typing exercises.							
18. Shows stamina and fitness in physical activities.							
19. Shows a good sense of balance and agility.							
20. Cooperates well as a member of a team.							

Fig. 3.14: Market Weighton School's Profile based on the Evesham Profile

	COMMUNICATION SKILLS	STAFF SIGNATURE & DATE	STAMP
1	CAN WRITE EFFECTIVELY AND CLEARLY		
2	CAN APPLY THE CONVENTIONAL RULES OF PUNCTUATION AND SPELLING		
3	HAS LEGIBLE HANDWRITING		
4	CAN SELECT AND USE THE APPROPRIATE STYLE OF LETTER WRITING		
5	CAN ACCURATELY COMPLETE A STANDARD FORM		
6	CAN RECEIVE AND UNDERSTAND SIMPLE SPOKEN MESSAGES		
7	CAN GIVE A CLEAR ORAL REPORT		
8	CAN ACT UPON GIVEN INSTRUCTION		
9	CAN CONVEY SIMPLE DIRECTIONS EFFECTIVELY		
10	CAN READ AND COMPREHEND AT LEAST AT THE LEVEL OF A POPULAR NEWSPAPER		
11	CAN EFFECTIVELY USE COMMON RETRIEVAL SYSTEM		
12	CAN UNDERSTAND SIMPLE TABULAR AND GRAPHICAL MATERIAL IN VARIOUS FORMS		
13	UNDERSTANDS A CERTAIN AMOUNT OF CONVERSATIONAL	FRENCH	
14	SPEAKS A CERTAIN AMOUNT OF CONVERSATIONAL	FRENCH	
15	CAN WRITE A CERTAIN OF	FRENCH	
16	CAN DEMONSTRATE CAPACITY TO MAKE INFORMED JUDGEMENT		
17	CAN DETECT BIAS IN PIECE OF WRITING OR IN SPEECH OR IN THE MEDIA		

	PERSONAL AND SOCIAL QUALITIES	STAFF SIGNATURE & DATE (Term 1, Term 2, Term 3, Term 1, Term 2, Term 3)	STAMP
1	HAS A GOOD ATTENDANCE RECORD		
2	IS NORMALLY PUNCTUAL		
3	IS NORMALLY PLEASANT AND WELL-MANNERED		
4	TAKES PRIDE IN HIS/HER APPEARANCE		
5	CAN ORGANISE HIS/HER WORK EFFICIENTLY		
6	CAN WORK WELL WITHOUT SUPERVISION		
7	CAN WORK WELL AS A MEMBER OF A GROUP		
8	HAS SHOWN INITIATIVE		
9	SHOWS CAPACITY FOR LEADERSHIP		
10	SHOWS A CAPACITY FOR ORGANISATION		
11	HAS HELD A POSITION OF RESPONSIBILITY IN SCHOOL		
12	HAS SHOWN RESPONSIBILITY IN HIS/HER ATTITUDE TOWARDS SCHOOL		
13	REACTS FAVOURABLY TO AUTHORITY		
14	RELATES WELL TOWARDS FELLOW PUPILS		
15	IS COURTEOUS AND SHOWS CONSIDERATION FOR OTHERS		

Fig. 3.15: Dean Magna School's Profile based on the Evesham Profile

to offer more information to employers. It is called the Personal Achievement Record (PAR) and is a small, pocket-sized log book which students can carry around. It is made up of four equal areas: Mathematics, Language, Practical Skills, Personal and Social Skills. Each area has twenty skills, which can be validated by the teacher (see Fig. 3.13). In this scheme it is entirely the student's responsibility to look after the log book and to approach the teacher for validation. This is effected by endorsing a particular skill with a rubber stamp (a forgery-proof stamp might help!).

Since introducing the PAR the school has been inundated with hundreds of nationwide requests for information, and many schools, in particular, have implemented it either as it stands or in an adapted format (see Figs. 3.14 and 3.15).

Perhaps one reason for its popularity is that it is the profile system which involves least disruption to the existing system – much of the testing required to establish mastery of a specific skill can be undertaken in normal lesson time, and teachers are merely required to stamp a card – far less time-consuming than written comments.

Profiling takes place in the 5th year only – in common with many schemes – it is only as experience of profiling is accrued that many people are realising the advantages of extending the process down the school, and it is now not uncommon to hear it being mooted as beneficial from the 1st year onwards.[8]

b. RSA practical profile schemes

The most influential example of a public body using a criterion checklist profile is the Royal Society of Arts Examination Board. It offers a series of profiles for communication skills, numeracy skills, practical skills, vocational preparation (clerical and distribution) and the most recent addition is the development of a general profile, incorporating communication, numeracy and practical skills.

Profile certificates are awarded by the RSA and can be used for a wide range of courses in schools, colleges, training centres and adult education. These profiles therefore cover a very wide age and ability range. Certificates consist of two parts: the course description and the profile statement. The profile statement is a collection of profile sentences (see Fig. 3.16).

Both the skills and the learning experiences to be assessed are checklisted. When the teacher is convinced that the student has mastered a specific skill, credit is given by marking a skills record sheet (see Fig. 3.17).

Because the RSA profile is not prescriptive it offers teachers considerable flexibility in the writing of assignments. On the other hand it does provide a structure; the outcome is flexibility within a framework.

The process of dialogue and negotiation between teacher and student is important. Information is transferred to a Continuous Assessment Record Sheet (see Fig. 3.17) and submitted to the RSA.

The profile certificates are prepared from this information. An important part is played by the external assessor who offers advice, liaises with the Board

and other centres and ensures those credits are justified. Only positive statements are included in the profile certificate. RSA profile certificates are widely
used in the FE sector, whose representatives have been very influential in
developing the profiles.

It is only comparatively recently that schools have been encouraged to participate, and the fact that many schools now offer RSA profiles is largely due to
the pioneering efforts of Hayesfield School, Bath. The school persuaded RSA
that they were able to offer (initially) a Vocational Preparation (Clerical) course
which would fulfil the criteria of a realistic, participative and negotiated
curriculum together with varied work experience.

Their success has paved the way for other schools to adopt RSA profiles;
further courses have been introduced and the numbers opting for them have
increased annually.

There is a considerable effect on the curriculum in that assignments have
to be written which will enable students to experience specific learning activities, to acquire specific skills and to incorporate these into an integrated
course.

c. Some participants' views of criterion checklists
Evesham
There has been considerable liaison with and support from local employers
who contributed both financially and in the development of the profile. Most
local employers ask to see the PAR at interviews – the implication is that
employers find it useful.

Most staff are enthusiastic – one tutor said: 'It promotes the motivation of
pupils by introducing formal accreditation for a wide range of achievements.'
One teacher felt that the effect of the PAR was so beneficial that it should be
extended: 'I would like to have a space for comments; it means extra work,
but if we're going to have it, we might as well do profiling properly'; whilst
another highlighted one of the problems of the checklist approach: 'If you fill
in "avoids elementary spelling mistakes" for the lowest ability, the most able
should have everything stamped.'

Pupils are generally enthusiastic about the PARs – this is demonstrated by
the fact that participation is voluntary, and the vast majority of pupils take up
the option (92% in 1984/5). Individual responses included: 'I like the fact that
it's our choice whether we take part, and it's our responsibility', and: 'It helps
with interviews – it presents an instant image of you, and starts conversation.'
One perceptive participant commented: 'It helps you take more interest in your
work – gives you something to go for – in the 4th year it's only work, it would
add interest if it could be used in the 4th and the 5th year.' (The same system
of credits as motivators and measurements of skill has now been extended to
the 4th year.)
Hayesfield
It is obvious from observation of the youngsters at work, and from discussion,
that they enjoy the course, and value the profile certificate. One reason,

Practical Communication Skills Profile

The Student has demonstrated the ability to:

A   *Dealing with People*

1.   establish working relationships with individuals
2.   establish working relationships as a member of a group
3.   relay given information orally to an individual
4.   relay given information orally to a group
5.   ask questions in order to gain information for a specific purpose
6.   make and carry out arrangements (in accordance with a stated goal)
7.   give instructions (in order that a particular task can be completed)
8.   take instructions (in order that a particular task can be completed)
9.   describe an object, person or event (so that it can be recognised and appreciated)
10. explain a process or sequence of events (so that it can be followed)
11. open, conduct and close a brief transaction (in accordance with a stated purpose)
12. open, conduct and close a brief transaction (in accordance with a stated purpose) by telephone
13. listen to each point of view presented in discussion and when asked re-state it accurately
14. state own point of view in a discussion (clearly and appropriately)
15. distinguish fact from opinion during a discussion
16. judge the validity of arguments presented in discussion
17. express disagreement without provoking hostility in discussion
18. participate effectively in the negotiation of a possible course of action.

B   *Dealing with Information*

1.   read straightforward printed texts (and extract the information required)
2.   read straightforward handwritten texts (and extract the information required)
3.   read a short article, letter or detailed notice in printed form (and extract information required)
4.   read a short article, letter or detailed notice in clear handwritten form (and extract information required)
5.   read texts containing complex sentences or sophisticated vocabulary in either handwritten or printed form
6.   scan written material and locate a required item
7.   skim written material and convey the gist
8.   use alphabetical order and index systems and locate desired information in dictionaries, directories and reference books
9.   ¹locate information in a library or filing system (to be used for a stated purpose)
10. copy accurately (so that information transferred is the same as the original)
11. check written material for errors and discrepancies
12. interpret and make use of pictorial and graphic information such as pictures, diagrams, graphs, tables, maps, dials, gauges*
13. present information in pictorial or graphic form (so that it can be acted upon)
14. make notes from written and spoken material (for a specific purpose)
15. relay accurately a given piece of spoken information in writing
16. adapt a given piece of information (into an appropriate format for a stated purpose)

17. use appropriate content and expression in writing
18. produce a simple report of a given situation or event (in order that the essential facts are conveyed to others)
19. produce everyday letters (both formal and informal, in order to achieve stated response)
20. complete accurately and legibly a variety of forms
21. carry out everyday financial transactions (in order to receive or transfer money through cheques, giros, etc)
22. file course work and records systematically (so that a specific item can be easily located)
23. retrieve information from computer based sources (e.g. viewdata, teletext, word processors)

*Students should show evidence in at least four of the suggested media for this sentence to be credited.

Note

Items inside the brackets appear for teachers, but not on the profile certificates.

Fig. 3.16: An RSA profile statement

suggested by a teacher, is that the profile is positive – it only contains sentences saying what a youngster *can* do.

Another reason for the popularity of the checklist profile with staff teaching the course is that the curriculum is closely linked with assessment, and with credits being accumulated throughout the year, students are motivated to achieve higher standards.

The response of one teacher was illuminating. She said: 'I'm so happy – I didn't know I could be so happy teaching – it's revolutionised the way I teach throughout the school.'

One explanation offered for the marked staff satisfaction with the course could be the fairly instantaneous effect upon students; as a result of the formative element of the work, staff and students are constantly in touch with the improvements which the student is making.

d. Advantages of criterion checklists

i. Criterion checklists allow the student to demonstrate mastery of a specific skill without reference to the rest of the group.
ii. This inevitably avoids the ranking implicit in norm-referenced assessment, where students are placed in rank order within the group.
iii. A readily assimilated list of competences in an easily understood format can be devised.
iv. Biased assessments due to subjectivity can be minimised by the requirement for evidence that a specific skill has been mastered.
v. Depending upon the method adopted, criterion checklists may provide a method of profiling which is less time-consuming than many.

e. Disadvantages of criterion checklists

i. Brevity may lead to meaningless or ambiguous criteria, but there is a danger of the profile becoming unwieldy if the list of statements is expanded.

ROYAL SOCIETY OF ARTS EXAMINATIONS BOARD
PRACTICAL COMMUNICATION PROFILE
SKILLS RECORD SHEET

Place ✓ in the box where skills have been demonstrated according to the checklisting for the assignment, otherwise leave empty.

Student ..C̲L̲A̲I̲R̲.̲ B̲A̲K̲E̲R̲..............   Tutor ....

SKILLS — TASK AND DATE / DEALING WITH PEOPLE	MULTI-CULTURE	WORK EXPERIENCE SECTION IA	SECTION IB	SECTION 2	COMMUNITY SERVICE	BURROWNN IN THE HOME	TUTOR TIME	LEISURE	SUPP. PREP. FOR TUT.
A1 Establishing working relationships with individuals	✓				?		✓	✓	
A2 Establishing working relationships as a member of a group	?				?		✓	✓	
A3 Relaying given information orally to an individual	?				?		✓	✓	
A4 Relaying given information orally to a group	?						✓		✓
A5 Asking questions	✓	✓			O		✓	✓	
A6 Making, carrying out arrangements				✓	?		✓	✓	
A7 Giving instructions					?		✓		✓
A8 Responding to instructions	✓			✓	✓	✓	✓	✓	
A9 Giving descriptions	?						✓	✓	
A10 Giving explanations					O		?		
A11 Opening/conducting brief transactions					O		✓		
A12 Opening/conducting brief transactions by telephone							✓		
A13 Listening to points of view in discussion and restating							✓		
A14 Contributing own point of view in discussion							?	?	
A15 Distinguishing fact from opinion in discussion							?		
A16 Evaluating arguments in discussion							?		
A17 Expressing disagreement in discussion							?✓		
A18 Participating in negotiation of course of action							✓	✓	

Fig. 3.17: An RSA Continuous Assessment Record Sheet completed by Hayesfield School

DEALING WITH INFORMATION / TASK AND DATE	SECTION 1A	SECTION 1B	SECTION 2	CON. SERVICE	SUBJOURN IN THE HOME	PREP FOR TURN(SUPP?)			
B1 Reading straight forward printed texts to extract information	✓	✓✓		✓	?	✓			
B2 Reading straight forward hand-written texts to extract information		✓			✓	✓			
B3 Reading moderately detailed printed texts to extract information	?	✓		✓	?	✓			
B4 Reading moderately detailed hand-written texts to extract information		✓			✓	✓			
B5 Reading complex texts to extract information									
B6 Scanning written material	?	✓✓		✓		✓			
B7 Skimming written material									
B8 Using dictionaries, directories and reference books						✓			
B9 Locating information in library or filing system	✓								
B10 Copying accurately	✓	✓		✓	O	✓			
B11 Checking for discrepancies			✓	✓✓	O	✓			
B12 Interpreting and using pictorial and graphic information	?			✓		✓			
B13 Presenting pictorial and graphic information	?			✓		✓			
B14 Taking notes		?							
B15 Relaying spoken information in writing		?							
B16 Adapting information		?✓		✓		✓			
B17 Using appropriate content and expression	✓					✓			
B18 Writing reports		O				?	?		
B19 Writing letters						✓			
B20 Completing forms		✓✓	✓	✓		✓			
B21 Carrying out everyday financial transactions									
B22 Filing course work and records		✓✓		✓					
B23 Retrieve information from computer based sources									

ii. With the inclusion of only one level of competence for a specific skill, the
level may be too high for some and too low for others, offering a poor
learning target.

iii. This makes the criterion checklist less suitable for profiling activity across
the whole ability range.

iv. Whilst in some cases the formative interaction of student and teacher is
encouraged, it is not built in to the infrastructure.

f. Summary for potential users of criterion checklists

It is obvious from this section that criterion checklists have been influential
in the growth of the profiles movement in recent years. They have proved
popular both in schools and in colleges. There is, however, a far smaller formative component inherent in the system than in, say, personal recording.

If your organisation seeks either a simple document which may be implemented into an existing system, without demanding a radical review of the
whole curriculum, or a profile certificate which can credit skills within a
course, then the models reviewed under criterion checklists may satisfy this
need.

If, however, you wish to institute a reform of the curriculum, and a reform
of the reporting/recording system, then existing samples of criterion checklists
may not be suitable. It also appears to be very difficult to devise a criterion
checklist profile which is equally appropriate for the whole ability range.

It is, however, worth remembering that RSA courses and profiles have
proved valuable motivators for a significant target group, and that many
schools have found the approach sufficiently attractive to adopt it. It may be
that some of the more attractive characteristics could be adapted to meet your
needs.

3.4   Comment banks (see also 7.10)

Whereas grid-style profiles (3.5) originate from some of the earliest attempts
at profiling, comment banks illustrate the most recent development. In an
attempt to counteract some of the perceived disadvantages of grids, there has
been a move, notably in Wales, to develop a system which offers teachers a
'bank' of standardised comments from which they may select in order to form
appropriate descriptions of students.

Initially, areas to be assessed must be agreed; the next stage is the compilation
of the bank of comments (usually between ten and twenty for each area). It
is possible to employ either open or closed banks – if closed, teachers must
select only from the available comments; if open, they may substitute their own
comments if necessary.

The comments are numbered to facilitate teacher selection and reduce
administrative time: the numbers are then transcribed into written descriptions
by clerical staff.

The objective is to produce an individualised, written statement about each student, whilst ensuring some degree of comparability between staff and avoiding both the giant steps and the ranking inherent in grids.

Comment banks bear a close resemblance to criterion checklists; the essential difference is that criterion checklists require mastery of predetermined levels of skills, and are frequently presented as lists of profile sentences in a 'can-do' form. Comment banks are not limited to specific skills objectives – they can also include personal characteristics, and are presented in the form of continuous prose, so that the student receives a statement which is tailored to the individual, whilst a degree of comparability is assured by the fact that teachers all choose from the same range of comments.

a. Clwyd

The Clwyd pilot scheme was influential in developing this model – four schools in Clwyd combined to produce a joint scheme. The LEA supported the pilot to the extent of providing a half-time teacher to each school, clerical assistance and generous cover to enable staff from all four schools to meet, develop the list of comments and liaise over implementation. Head teachers from two of the schools were seconded for one year on related projects (see Fig. 3.18).

b. Welsh profile

In November 1980 the Schools Council Committee for Wales and the Welsh Joint Education Committee funded a feasibility study on methods of profile reporting. A proposed pilot scheme was published in November 1983,[9] based upon the comment bank approach.

The principle is very similar to that described earlier in this section. Areas to be assessed include:

Attitude to people
Attitude to work in school
Attitude to school activities

Oral communication
Written communication
Graphic communication

Practical skills
Numerical skills

Examples of the way in which these comments may be translated into statements is offered in the Welsh model (see Fig. 3.19).

A unique feature of this profile is that it is the first national profile to be introduced. It is, admittedly, far easier to administer a national profile under the Welsh education system than under the English, but it will nevertheless provide valuable insights into the practicality and desirability of instituting a national scheme.

BANKS OF COMMENTS   LITERACY

1.   VARIETY OR RANGE OF WRITTEN WORK

A1.   .....has the ability to use the appropriate style for both imaginative
       and formal writing.

A2.   His/her imaginative writing is fluent and original.

A3.   He/she can adopt an appropriate writing style for more formal assignments.

A4.   He/she can sometimes adopt the appropriate style for his/her writing.

2.   ORGANISATION OF WRITTEN WORK

B1.   .....demonstrates the ability to plan, prepare and organise his/her work.

B2.   He/she demonstrates some ability to plan work in advance.

B3.   .....can plan and organise simple pieces of work.

B4.   .....can organise his/her work according to a given plan.

3.   TECHNICAL SKILLS

C1.   He/she writes with a high degree of accuracy in spelling, punctuation and
       grammar.

C2.   He/she can achieve an acceptable standard of accuracy in spelling,
       punctuation and grammar.

C3.   He/she uses punctuation well to aid communication.

C4.   His/her writing is grammatically correct.

C5.   His/her spelling is accurate.

C6.   He/she can achieve a degree of accuracy in spelling, punctuation and
       grammar when assisted.

4.   READING COMPREHENSION

D1.   He/she can read easily a wide variety of written material showing clear
       evidence of understanding.

D2.   He/she can read certain types of written material showing clear evidence
       of understanding.

D3.   He/she can read and understand simple written material.

D4.   He/she can read and understand simple written material with assistance.

PROFILE STATEMENT

Literacy   Janet has the ability to use the appropriate style for both
            imaginative and formal writing, demonstrates the ability to
            plan, prepare and organise her work and can achieve an
            acceptable standard of accuracy in spelling, punctuation and
            grammar. She can read easily a wide variety of written material
            showing clear evidence of understanding and can select relevant
            material from a given source of information. She can respond with
            sensitivity to the emotions and ideas conveyed by a writer and
            listens attentively to others in a variety of situations and,
            when appropriate, for long periods.

Fig. 3.18: The Clwyd pilot scheme

Personal Qualities

Sian is able to form and maintain very good relationships with adults and pupils, although some encouragement is needed in the first instance. If called upon she has shown that she can act as an organiser but she prefers not to take a leading role.

Even in the face of difficulties Sian's perseverance and application are notable and very little supervision is needed to enable her to complete work. Homework tasks are completed regularly and usually satisfactorily.

When encouraged Sian participates reliably and conscientiously in school activities and she has shown loyalty and commitment to the school on many occasions.

Personal Qualities

Huw is able to get on well with most pupils but prefers not to take a leading role. He needs constant encouragement to relate to others although he is well mannered and courteous and is generally accepted by most adults.

Huw perseveres with most tasks although some encouragement is needed in the face of difficulties. Homework tasks are completed regularly and usually satisfactorily, but work is not always organised effectively unless advice is given. Although he tries to present work neatly he does not always succeed in doing so.

He is well behaved in class but has shown little desire to become involved in the extra-curricular life of the school. He takes part in the occasional school activity when his interest is captured but his main interests lie outside school.

Communication Skills

Sian speaks readily in a small group but is more reluctant to contribute orally during class. She speaks clearly and usually correctly.

Sian can research and organise most information effectively and most written material can be read and understood. She has a feeling for language and uses an appropriate style of writing. Her command of vocabulary is good and she spells and punctuates with acceptable accuracy for most purposes.

Sian can interpret intricate plans, maps, patterns and diagrams. She can select the appropriate form of representation and is able to draw simple diagrams accurately.

Communication Skills

Huw speaks readily in a small group but is more reluctant to contribute orally in class.

Huw can read and understand most simple written material. He can look up information using an index and can extract straightforward facts. His vocabulary is basic but adequate for everyday communication and he can spell and punctuate simple sentences.

Huw can interpret simple plans and diagrams and is able to sketch simple diagrams which do not call for accurate use of scale.

Fig. 3.19: The Welsh profile

c. Comment banks in practice

Effective organisation is essential in a complex procedure involving all 5th year pupils. In order to achieve this, in one Clwyd school (Deeside High School, Clwyd):

  i. Teachers adopt a rolling programme of systematic observation of and discussion with children.
 ii. Each tutor is allocated half an hour per morning plus one tutor period for profiling activities.
iii. A series of dates for completion of assessments is published at the beginning of the year.

Assessment is not subject-based, but cross-curricular.

Final statements are typewritten into a final leaving certificate, and in order that all students, regardless of ability, may enjoy a moment of glory, the profiles are presented at a special leaving ceremony.

d. Some participants' views of comment banks: Deeside High School

After some years of examining existing assessment procedures, and as a result of his conviction that every child is entitled to a full professional evaluation of activities in which they have been engaged, the head of one of the pilot schools became committed to the concept of profiles based on comment banks in 1978.

One particularly important factor in the new scheme was a belief that profiles (and any other significant curriculum innovation) should emanate from the body of the staff, rather than be an externally imposed addition (which raises questions regarding the efficacy of a national profile). He also believed in dialogue between students and teachers, rather than an atmosphere of 'instruction'.

The school takes the student's self-development and right to receive credit for achievement as the central focus for the profile, rather than any potential use by employers. One teacher mentioned that profiles '. . . help me to know my tutor group better because I make an attempt to talk to pupils on a systematic basis'. Another teacher said that 'Feedback from pupils indicates that the profile is a motivating factor – not stupendous, but definite, particularly for those who were turned off by academic work!'. Teachers on the whole liked the comment bank system, partly because it reduced actual writing time – one warning voice stated: 'If the work is not realistic in terms of teacher time and inset, it will not happen.'

e. Advantages of comment banks

  i. Labelling students can be avoided.
 ii. There is no suggestion of grading in the final personalised statement.
iii. Norm-referencing and the normal curve of distribution can be avoided.
 iv. Young people are presented with a series of positive statements in clear English.

v. Comment banks ensure a greater degree of comparability between teachers than is possible in free response.

vi. A wider, and more accurate range of expression, terminology and vocabulary is made available than that usually found in the traditional school report.

vii. The system ensures that any negative comments are neither defamatory or condemnatory.

viii. The system is administratively convenient.

f. Disadvantages of comment banks

i. Although norm-referencing may be avoided, unless the quality of the *statements* is secured, comments may be as implicitly norming as the old A–E grades when presented as a hierarchical list of statements.

ii. Reliability between schools depends on consensus procedures and highly specific comments.

iii. There may be little indication of what the student is *not* capable of – a possible disadvantage for employers.

iv. If teachers and users become so familiar with the list of statements, profiles may become as stereotyped as the old system of school reports.

v. In spite of claims to the contrary, the use of comment banks appears to lean heavily towards the summative end of the formative → summative continuum.

g. Summary for potential users of comment banks

It is still early days for comment banks. There is undoubtedly a considerable amount of work to be done on developing and refining the process.

If you want a profile system which provides students with an individualised statement of achievements, qualities and abilities, which does not record a composite mark for a particular area, does not imply a pass or fail, does not compare one pupil with another and is compatible with computer assisted profiling, then comment banks may well make a valuable contribution.

However, in addition to some of the disadvantages discussed earlier, it does appear that many users have not really incorporated a truly formative element into the comment bank system. In its present form it is, despite the praiseworthy motives of its instigators, still something which is again 'done to pupils by teachers'. The Avon Student Profile attempts to use comment banks in a formative way, but it remains to be seen whether this works in practice.

3.5 Grid-style profiles (see also 7.10)

These are probably the most familiar of the profile recording styles. The name provides a clue to the method of recording, which involves the grading of skill-based criteria upon a grid. An essential feature of grids is that they assume hierarchical learning, which is frequently not what happens in practice.

The number of levels used on the grid varies between three and six, as shown in the diagram below.[10]

Skills

Listening		*Speaking*	
Acts independently and intelligently on complex verbal instructions	☐	Can debate a point of view	☐
Can interpret and act on most complex instructions	☐	Can make a clear and accurate oral report	☐
Can interpret and act on straightforward instructions	☐	Can describe events orally	☐
Can carry out simple instructions with supervision	☐	Can communicate adequately at conversation level	☐

It is a common feature of grid-style profiles that skills replace traditional subject categories (although this is not confined solely to grids) and there is assessment of cross-curricular skills such as 'listening', 'problem-solving', etc.

The Scottish Council for Research in Education (SCRE) developed a pioneering grid-style profile for schools in 1977, after several years of research and development.[11] This was closely followed by the FEU[12]; the FEU model was then refined and developed by City and Guilds of London Institute. It is clear that these have been powerful and influential bodies involved in the development of grids, but in recent years concern has been expressed about the desirability of an approach which may only be a refinement of the grade (A–E) system.[13]

A large number of individually devised grids are available, although it is significant that many mirror the categories established in the original SCRE profile (see Figs. 3.20, 3.21 and 3.22).

Two examples are chosen to consider in more detail: the SCRE grid is an example of a profile designed for schools, whilst the City and Guilds General Abilities Profile was originally designed for FE. This is now becoming more readily available in schools – another example of a profile spanning the school/FE divide.

a. Scottish Council for Research in Education (SCRE)

The SCRE initiated the idea of a profile in which basic skills, subject attainment and personal qualities are further broken down into components, giving a fuller and more detailed picture of a pupil's attributes and achievements in individual areas rather than a global 'C' for 'English'. In so doing it was hoped to give credit to youngsters for skills and achievements not recognised in traditional reports.

Teachers fill in a separate assessment record on each individual pupil;

LISTENING/SPEAKING

A	Listens well and can explain and discuss confidently and appropriately
B	Above average in listening and speaking
C	Adequate powers of listening and speaking, in small groups or one-to-one situation
D	Below average in listening and speaking
E	Has some difficulty in understanding speech and own speaking lacks clarity

WRITING

A	Can write accurately, fluently and lucidly on a range of subjects
B	Can write with clarity, effectiveness and acceptable accuracy
C	Can write with reasonable accuracy and fluency
D	Written expression intelligible but either inaccurate or very limited
E	Experiences difficulty with most aspects of written work

READING

A	A thoughtful and versatile reader, able to respond to complex material
B	Sound comprehension of ideas, facts and standard vocabulary
C	Able to understand most everyday written material
D	Only a limited understanding of everyday written material
E	Poor comprehension of everyday written material

USE OF NUMBER

A	Quick and accurate
B	Can handle routine calculations accurately with practice
C	Can barely cope with simple calculations

MATHEMATICAL REASONING

A	Logical and accurate
B	Copes with practice but needs help
C	Has great difficulty in reasoning logically

ATTENDANCE

A	Excellent and regular
B	Absent infrequently and only with good reason
C	Absent regularly but apparently with good reason
D	Irregular attendance for no good reason
E	Very poor attendance

PUNCTUALITY

A	Always on time
B	Late only with good reason
C	Shows some lack of dependability
D	Regularly late
E	Invariably late

APPEARANCE

A	Exemplary
B	Always in school dress
C	School dress normally worn
D	Neat but not in school dress
E	Little regard for neatness or school dress

MANNER & FRIENDSHIP

A	Self confident and sure. Capable of mature friendships
B	General bearing good, quite impressive
C	The average. Some self assurance, not nervous
D	Manner fair, only somewhat retiring. Difficulty in establishing relationships
E	Very shy and nervous, avoids others, something of a loner

ASSERTIVENESS

A	Very strong personality
B	Fairly self assertive
C	Dominant only when the occasion demands
D	Usually prefers to avoid the limelight
E	Passive, almost negative

Fig. 3.20: A grid-style profile from *Recording Achievement at 16+* by Brian Goacher

Full Name		Sex	Date of Birth	Secondary Schools attended	From	To

Address

Personal Qualities (please tick as appropriate)

RELIABILITY	Exceptionally reliable ☐	Not very reliable ☐	Reliable ☐
CO-OPERATIVENESS	Co-operative ☐	Exceptionally co-operative ☐	Not very co-operative ☐
ATTITUDES TO PEOPLE IN AUTHORITY	Has shown resentment ☐	Co-operative, always positive ☐	Accepts correction without resentment ☐
MANNER	Shy and nervous ☐	Somewhat retiring ☐	Self confident and sure ☐	Some self assurance, not nervous ☐
KEENNESS & INDUSTRY	Exceptionally industrious & keen ☐	Prepared to make some effort ☐	Gives up easily ☐	A good keen worker ☐
INITIATIVE	Needs pushing ☐	Fairly resourceful ☐	Prefers guidance ☐	Quick to seize opportunities & develop them ☐
SOCIABILITY	Popular with close friends ☐	Good mixer ☐	Prefers to work alone ☐	Does not get on with others ☐

Interests, Achievements and any other comments (use continuation sheet if necessary)

Attendance	Number of times late	Health

Main Subjects Studied	Exam	Ability	Result	Main Subjects Studied	Exam	Ability	Result

Other Subjects Studied

Signature of Validation _____   Headteacher _____

Position _____   Date _____

Fig. 3.21: The Halton Profile. An extract from the summative profile which is supported by extensive formative profiling

ATTAINMENTS IN BASIC ABILITIES				
COMMUNICATION	**(Basic Level)**			**(High Level)**
Talking and Listening	Can hold conversations with workmates. face-to-face or by phone.	Can follow and give simple descriptions and explanations. Can take messages.	Can communicate effectively with a range of people in a variety of situations.	Can present a logical and effective argument. Can analyse others' arguments.
1				
Reading and Writing	Can understand and write simple notices. labels and short notes.	Can follow and give straightforward written instructions and explanations.	Can use instruction manuals and can write reports describing work done.	Can select and criticise written data and use it to produce own written work.
2				
Visual Understanding	Can interpret simple signs and indicators.	Can, after guidance, make use of basic graphs, charts, tables, drawings etc.	Can interpret and use basic graphs, charts, tables and drawings unaided.	Can construct graphs etc, and extract information to support arguments.
3				
PRACTICAL AND NUMERICAL ABILITIES				
Using Equipment	After demonstration, can use equipment safely to perform simple tasks.	With guidance, can use equipment safely to perform multi-step tasks.	Can select and use suitable equipment and materials for the job, without help.	Can set up and maintain equipment. Can identify/remedy common faults.
7				
Dexterity and Co-ordination	Can use everyday implements; can lift, carry and set down objects as directed.	Can reliably perform basic manipulative tasks.	Can perform complex tasks requiring accuracy and dexterity.	Can perform tasks requiring a high degree of manipulation control.
8				
Measuring	Can read graduated linear scales and dials.	Can measure out specified quantities of material by length, weight etc.	Can set up and use simple precision instruments.	Can set up and use complex precision instruments.
9				
Calculating	Can identify size, shape, order etc. Can add and subtract whole numbers.	Can use $- / - / \times / -$ to solve single-step, whole number problems. Can estimate.	Can use $- / - / \times / -$ to solve two-step problems. Can add and subtract decimals.	Can use $+ / - / \times / -$ to solve multi-step problems. Can multiply and divide decimals.
10				

Fig. 3.22: Humberside LEA pilot profile for sixteen- to seventeen-year-old students (1980/81)

records for the whole class are mounted on a pegboard and results are transferred to a class assessment sheet.

The aim is that assessments should be carried out twice a year during the final years of schooling, and that these assessments should form the basis of the 'School Leaving Record' (see Fig. 3.23).

It is interesting that as recently as 1977 when the scheme was launched, and in spite of the laudable aims of the team responsible for its design, there was no provision for student participation – it was still very much something 'done to pupils by teachers' albeit with the aim of providing a more just and complete picture of the youngster.

b. City and Guilds General Abilities Profile
This profile, developed by an Examinations Board, is now one of the most widely used grid profiles (and probably the most widely used of any type of profile) (see Figs. 3.24 and 3.25).

The profile is allied to the CGLI 365 course, which is an integrated general and vocational preparation course including a common core and between three

SCHOOL LEAVING REPORT

This is a brief report on Queenie Quarry

Date of Birth: 13/7/1960

who completed class S4

in Tanochbrae High School

and left on 3rd July 1976

This report is the result of continuous assessment by all the teachers of this pupil and has the authority of:—

E. R. Smith Head Teacher

Director

OTHER OBSERVATIONS

(includes other school activities, other awards and comments on positive personal qualities).

Royal Life-Saving Society - Bronze Medallion

Member School Photographic Club, School Debating Society

Member of School Skiing trip to Austria Jan 1976

She has been resourceful in finding costumes for the school play.

She has recently shown an appreciation and enjoyment of literature and has read widely outside the syllabus.

Works well on group activities; gets on well with both pupils and teachers. Readily accepts responsibility, particularly in social activities.

Notes

The grades A–D represent approximately 25% of the year group in each case.

The skill gradings represent a consensus derived from the individual ratings of each teacher's knowledge and reflect the standard obtained by the pupil with reasonable consistency.

All the information contained in this report is based on profile assessments contributed by each teacher on a continuous and cumulative basis, including observations of personal qualities and informal activities.

© 1976 SCRE

(pages 1 and 4)

Fig. 3.23: SCRE Profile Assessment System

SKILLS

LISTENING
- Acts independently and intelligently on complex verbal instructions [TH]
- Can interpret and act on most complex instructions
- Can interpret and act on straightforward instructions
- Can carry out simple instructions with supervision

SPEAKING
- Can debate a point of view
- Can make a clear and accurate oral report [TH]
- Can describe events orally
- Can communicate adequately at conversation level

READING
- Understands all appropriate written material [TH]
- Understands the content and implications of most writing if simply expressed [TH]
- Understands uncomplicated ideas expressed in simple language
- Can read most everyday information such as notices or simple instructions

WRITING
- Can argue a point of view in writing
- Can write a clear and accurate report [TH]
- Can write a simple account or letter
- Can write simple messages and instructions

VISUAL UNDERSTANDING AND EXPRESSION
- Can communicate complex visual concepts readily and appropriately
- Can give a clear explanation by sketches and diagrams
- Can interpret a variety of visual displays such as graphs or train timetables
- Can interpret single visual displays such as roadsigns or outline maps

USE OF NUMBER
- Quick and accurate in complicated or unfamiliar calculations [TH]
- Can do familiar or straightforward calculations, more slowly if complex
- Can handle routine calculations with practice [TH]
- Can do simple whole number calculations such as giving change

MANUAL DEXTERITY
- Has fine control of complex tools and equipment
- Satisfactory use of most tools and equipment
- Can achieve simple tasks such as wiring a plug [TH]
- Can use simple tools, instruments and machines such as a screwdriver

PHYSICAL CO-ORDINATION
- A natural flair for complex tasks
- Mastery of a wide variety of movements
- Can perform satisfactorily most everyday movements
- Can perform simple physical skills such as lifting or climbing

SUBJECT/ACTIVITY ASSESSMENT

Curriculum Area	Subjects Studied (includes final year level where relevant)	Years of Study	Achievement	Enterprise (includes flair, creativity)	Perseverance (includes reliability, carefulness)
Aesthetic Subjects	Drawing	1–4	2	2	1
	Music	1–4	2	3	3
Business Studies					
Community/Leisure Activities	Social Education	1–4	3	2	3
Crafts	Pottery	3–4	2	1	3
English	English	1–4	2	1	3
Mathematics	Arithmetic	1–4	1	1	2
Other Languages	German	2–4	2	2	3
Outdoor Studies	Outdoor Pursuits	3–4	2	2	3
Physical Education	General	1–4	3	1	3
Science	Biology	3–4	1	2	2
Social Subjects	History	1–4	2	1	3

(pages 2 and 3)

CITY AND GUILDS OF LONDON INSTITUTE

<u>365 VOCATIONAL PREPARATION (GENERAL)</u>

ATTAINMENTS IN BASIC ABILITIES

		(Basic Level)				(High Level)
COMMUNICATION	TALKING AND LISTENING	Can make sensible replies when spoken to	Can hold conversations and can take messages	Can follow and give simple descriptions and explanations	Can communicate effectively with a range of people in a variety of situations	Can present a logical and effective argument. Can analyse others' arguments
	READING	Can read words and short phrases	Can read straight-forward messages	Can follow straight-forward instructions and explanations	Can understand a variety of forms of written materials	Can select and judge written materials to support an argument
	WRITING	Can write words and short phrases	Can write straight-forward messages	Can write straight-forward instructions and explanations	Can write reports describing work done	Can write a critical analysis, using a variety of sources
	USING SIGNS AND DIAGRAMS	Can recognise everyday signs and symbols	Can make use of simple drawings, maps, timetables	Can make use of basic graphs, charts, codes, technical drawings, with help	Can interpret and use basic graphs, charts, technical drawings unaided	Can construct graphs and extract information to support conclusions
	COMPUTER APPRECIATION	Can recognise everyday uses of computers	Can use keyboard to gain access to data	Can enter data into the system using existing programs	Can identify potential applications for computers	Can construct error free programs
PRACTICAL & NUMERICAL	SAFETY	Can explain the need for safety rules	Can remember safety instructions	Can spot safety hazards	Can apply safe working practices independently	Can maintain, and suggest improve-ments to, safety measures
	USING EQUIPMENT	Can use equipment safely to perform simple tasks under guidance	Can use equipment safely to perform a sequence of tasks after demonstration	Can select and use suitable equipment and materials for the job, without help	Can set up and use equipment to produce work to standard	Can identify and remedy common faults in equipment
	NUMERACY	Can count objects	Can solve problems by adding and subtracting	Can solve problems by multiplying and dividing	Can calculate ratios, percentages and proportions	Can use algebraic formulae
SOCIAL	WORKING IN A GROUP	Can cooperate with others when asked	Can work with other members of the group to achieve common aims	Can understand own position and results of own actions within a group	Can be an active and decisive member of a group	Can adopt a variety of roles in a group
	ACCEPTING RESPONSIBILITY	Can follow instructions for simple tasks and carry them out under guidance	Can follow instructions for simple tasks and carry them out independently	Can follow a series of instructions and carry them out independently	Can perform a variety of tasks effectively given minimal guidance	Can assume responsibility for delegated tasks and take initiative
DECISION MAKING	PLANNING	Can identify the sequence of steps in everyday tasks, with prompting	Can describe the sequence of steps in a routine task, after demonstration	Can choose from given alternatives the best way of tackling a task	Can modify/extend given plans/routines to meet changed circumstances	Can create new plans/routines from scratch
	OBTAINING INFORMATION	Can ask for needed information	Can find needed information, with guidance	Can use standard sources of information	Can extract and assemble information from several given sources	Can show initiative in seeking and gathering infor-mation from a wide variety of sources
	COPING	Can cope with everyday activities, with help	Can cope with everyday problems. Seeks help if needed	Can cope with changes in familiar routines	Can cope with unexpected or unusual situations	Can help others to solve problems

Fig. 3.24

Sheet 1

CITY AND GUILDS OF LONDON INSTITUTE

365 VOCATIONAL PREPARATION (GENERAL)

EXAMPLES OF BASIC ABILITIES DEMONSTRATED ON THE COURSE

Topic/integrated Assignment INTRODUCTION TO THE MAKING OF THE LAW
(What laws would you make in an enclosed society?)

COMMUNICATION

1. Talking and listening Darren made a strong contribution to discussion. He was able to make his views known clearly and was a positive listener to others.

2. Reading The level of reading was demanding. Darren was able to show understanding of the complex ideas and concepts covered.

3. Writing A lot of writing was necessary. Darren took on a significant part of the role of writing up the findings of the group.

4. Using signs and diagrams A map of the 'island' was part of the group's work. Darren made useful contributions to the form and structure of the group's map.

5. Computer appreciation

PRACTICAL and NUMERICAL

6. Safety

7. Using equipment

8. Numeracy

SOCIAL

9. Working in a group Darren worked well as a member of this group. The work was essentially a cooperative exercise, his role was purposeful.

10. Accepting responsibility He took on the responsibility of finding library sources for the group and was a responsible member of the group generally.

DECISION MAKING

11. Planning Darren and his group made a well planned approach to the work and completed it to their own and my satisfaction.

12. Obtaining information Magazines and books were used to gain background to shipwrecks and the environments of desert islands

13. Coping There were setbacks, information was difficult to obtain, group members varied in their contributions. Darren coped with these situations well.

Signed D Smith (student)   Signed Jeff Hume (tutor)

Fig. 3.25: A profile completed by Portway School

```
CITY AND GUILDS PROFILE REPORT

PLEASANT HIGH SCHOOL

A. MOLE                    (Student)

N. STRATTON                (tutor)                        (C&G monitor)

COURSES
O level English
CSE mathematics
TVE Information technology
(etc)




MAIN ACTIVITIES

1 SHOOTING VIDEO
2 WORD-PROCESSING
3 BUSINESS REPORT
4 LEGAL ROLE-PLAY
5 COUNTING SHEEP
6 SHOP DISPLAY



* * * * * * * * * * * * * * * * * * * * * * * * * * * * * * * * * * * * * *


                    PROFILE  OF  ACHIEVEMENT   (Extract from
                                                  original)

TALKING & LISTENING

Can communicate effectively with a range of people in a variety of situations
e.g. Presented video film and talked to client about work being undertaken.

WRITING

Can write reports describing work done e.g. Reported on visit to fast food
establishment;  prepared menus and price list.

READING

Can understand a variety of forms of written materials e.g.  Has used
reference books, manuals, specimen documents & instruction sheets.

USING SIGNS & DIAGRAMS

Can make use of basic graphs, charts, codes technical drawings, with help
e.g. Followed diagrams to set up and operate video editing equipment.

COMPUTER APPRECIATION

Can enter data into the system using existing programs e.g. Word-processed
article for newsletter;  edited files.
```

Fig. 3.26

(student name)

USING EQUIPMENT

Can use equipment safely to perform a sequence of tasks after demonstration
e.g. Used electronic instruments & connected electronic devices in a circuit.

SAFETY

Can explain the need for safety rules e.g. Understands fire & accident
procedures at the school.

NUMERACY (2)

Can calculate percentages and averages e.g. Has used + - * / % when working
on sets of figures on business documents.

CREATING

Can produce a number of related ideas without help e.g. Designed a poster
advertising beans.

CLASSIFYING

Can use tree-like classifying systems e.g. Can work out tax benefits.

WORKING IN A GROUP

Can be active and decisive member of a group e.g. Helped plan shop
displays; role-played in legal situation.

WORKING WITH CLIENTS

Can anticipate and fulfil clients' needs from existing resources e.g. Built
up a spec. for video film by discussing it with client.

ACCEPTING RESPONSIBILITY

Can perform a variety of tasks effectively given minimal guidance e.g. Moved
stock (sheep); assessed forest machine limitations independently.

PLANNING

Can choose from given alternatives the best way of tackling a task e.g.
Planned layout of goods for a bakery shop.

OBTAINING INFORMATION

Can extract and assemble information from several given sources e.g. Carried
out a survey of the distance pupils travel to school.

ASSESSING OWN RESULTS

Can assess own results for familiar tasks, without help e.g. Filled in
accurate drafts of progress profiles.

COPING

Can cope with unexpected or unusual situations e.g. When herding sheep,
met another flock; sorted them out by organising two pens.

and five vocational options. Assessment consists of:
  i. Multiple choice tests
 ii. A record of experience and achievement
iii. A student progress profile
 iv. A final profile certificate.

City and Guilds sought to counter some of the problems associated with grids by incorporating a formative process of records, reviews (1–2 weekly) and progress profile reports (4–6 weekly) leading to the final end of course profile report. In each of these stages the student is actively involved in negotiation and completion of the profiles.

One drawback of the City and Guilds 365 profile is that it is course-centred rather than student-centred, and is not therefore suitable as a whole school profile. However, similar models which have been designed as student-centred profiles are in the process of piloting.

It is also envisaged that the final grid-style profile will evolve into a profile report which contains a course summary (Fig. 3.26) and statements, accompanied by examples of the student's best performance.

c. Grids in practice

The City and Guilds 365 course was offered for piloting in schools in 1983/4, and provided a good opportunity to study the effects of a profile system newly introduced into schools.

The fact that the profiles only related to one course meant that student numbers were limited, and that only a small group of teachers struggled with the concept of integrated cross-curricular courses and negotiated assessment.

In one school the numbers of pupils opting for the scheme dropped from fifteen to nine, which is barely viable in terms of pupil–teacher ratio, yet appeared to be about the optimum number in order for staff to be able to cope with the demands made of them. For instance, it had not been possible to maintain the recommended number of reviews and interim profiles.

This is not intended to be an evaluation of the course except in so far as it is relevant to the profile system, but it is worth noting that in spite of difficulties, the young people who had participated appeared to have gained in both confidence and attainment.

It is significant in terms of the formative–summative debate that the visit of the external assessor (examiner in their eyes) turned out to be a highlight. The act of sitting down with one person and discussing their progress and achievements appeared to be stimulating and satisfying.

City and Guilds' claim that there *is* scope for formative negotiation was borne out in discussions between individual students and tutor. Several points emerged clearly from this exercise:
  i. The high quality of tutoring must have played an essential part in the process of formative development.
 ii. Students' ability to make honest self-assessments were impressive – one lad said 'Yes, I'm lazy in that subject, leave that' contrasted with 'I think the

teacher is being a bit hard in this part – I used to find it difficult to mix but I'm much better now.'

iii. Students' objections to what they perceived as unfair assessments.
iv. The time-consuming nature of individual negotiation, yet:
v. The value in terms of personal development of such individual interviews.

d. Some participants' views of grids

There is insufficient evidence to produce an objective comparison between participants' views of grids and of other types of profile. In one of the new school pilot City and Guilds schemes, the following observation was made by a teacher, who said: 'It has meant tremendous improvement in my relationship with Kevin. He was so hostile initially that he wouldn't reveal anything about himself, but as he's become aware that the profile is intended to help *him*, and to look at him as a whole person, his attitude has completely changed.'

One of the youngsters, who had been isolated, withdrawn and lacking in confidence at the beginning of the year, stated that he had 'more confidence in myself. I can get on better with others.'

When asked about their reactions to the profile assessment, another boy, who had been something of a problem lower down the school, said 'it's much better, seeing all the things you can do, not like exams'. They also touched on the question of relationships saying that with some teachers it was difficult, but that 'Mr Hurran is really involved in how you are doing'.

The City and Guilds evaluation reinforces this point, quoting a teacher who said: 'They help deepen the relationship between the tutor and trainee. The trainee feels he is important and that someone is interested in him. He learns to appreciate what talents he has from their exposure on the grid.'[14]

It is however only fair to record contrary views – when one young person from another school was asked what he had done with his profile, he said 'burnt it!'.

e. Advantages of grid-style profiles

i. Easy to complete.
ii. Compact.
iii. Cover a wide range of skills, attitudes and qualities.
iv. Informative for users.
v. *Can* be progressive, in which case students are motivated to reach the next level.
vi. The information is presented in a compact and uniform manner, and in the case of shaded bars can be assimilated quickly.
vii. The approach is familiar to both teachers and employers.

f. Disadvantages of grid-style profiles

i. The steps between levels are often uneven.
ii. There is a danger that users will only consider the top level attainable and

overlook any lower levels of achievement.
iii. Although they appear to provide precise categories, they are often far from clear, e.g.

Learning Skills: Can learn in a limited range of contexts, with help[15]

iv. The giant steps involved in some grids make progression virtually impossible, e.g.

Skill Level	*Example*
Level 4 (basic)	Can climb a ladder
Level 1	Can assemble micro-circuits using a microscope[16]

v. Some skill categories are weakly defined, e.g.

Listening: acts indepently and intelligently on complex verbal instructions[17]

vi. There is a danger that teachers may exchange the straightjacket of examinations for the corset of grid category labels – an entirely opposite effect to the intention of the majority of profile pioneers.
vii. The temptation simply to tick boxes enhances the dangers of labelling and categorising students.

g. Summary for potential users of grid-style profiles

There is little doubt that grid-style profiles are now big business. They have the advantage of being compact, relatively easy to complete and familiar.

In the case of a course, such as City and Guilds 365, it is a feasible part of the whole package, but grid-style profiles may be less appropriate as an integral part of whole school assessment. (There are indications that City and Guilds are modifying their use of the grid in the final profile certificate.)

Take warning from the fact that the widely imitated SCRE model has largely lapsed into disuse in Scotland despite the thorough research and development programme.

If you do decide that grid-style profiles are the ones offering most to your institution, take great care that the formative possibilities inherent in profiling are not negated, that skill categories are very carefully defined and that the all-important process of teacher–student interaction, negotiation and participation are given sufficient weight.

Summary

This chapter has sought to identify and clarify the main approaches to recording assessments in profiling. The formative–summative debate has been a theme running throughout the chapter, and each type of profile format has been considered in relation to its formative or summative effect.

Whilst I have devised a model using five categories, it is possible, if you prefer, to adopt a different approach, using only two categories.

Who completes the profiles	– students (3.1A, 3.1B, 3.2)
	– students and teachers (3.2–3.5)
How do they do it	– free response (3.1A)
	– cumulative checklist (3.1B, 3.3, 3.4)
	– hierarchical grid (3.5)

There are no definitive answers to the question of which category is the 'ideal' profile. What is offered is a menu which, by listing the ingredients and discussing some of the issues relevant to each item, will facilitate selection of the most appropriate elements of profiles for each individual organisation.

Notes

1. Curriculum Study and Development Centre, Wiltshire, *The record of personal achievement: tutors' handbook*, Wiltshire County Council Education Department, 1974.
2. Stansbury, D., *Principles of personal recording*, The Springline Trust, 1984.
3. Swales, T., *Record of personal achievement; an independent evaluation of the Swindon RPA Scheme*, Schools Council, 1979.
4. Freshwater, M. and Oates, N., *Can-do cards and profiles: tools for self-assessment*, MSC, 1982.
5. Further Education Unit, *A basis for choice*, 1979.
6. Burgess, T. and Adams, E. (eds.), *Outcomes of education*, Macmillan, 1980.
7. Royal Society of Arts, *Practical skills profile schemes: communication. Notes for guidance*.
8. Department of Education and Science, and Welsh Office, *Records of achievement: a statement of policy*, 1984.
9. Schools Council Committee for Wales, *Profile reporting in Wales*, 1983.
10. Scottish Council for Research in Education, *Pupils in profile*, Hodder and Stoughton, 1977.
11. *Ibid.*
12. Further Education Unit, *A basis for choice*.
13. Scottish Vocational Preparation Unit, *Assessment in youth training: made to measure?*, Jordanhill School, 1982.
14. City and Guilds of London Institute, Validity of profiling; *experience of profiling*, 1983.
15. Further Education Unit, *A basis for choice*.
16. Scottish Vocational Preparation Unit, *Assessment in youth training*.
17. Scottish Council for Research in Education, *Pupils in profile*.

Chapter 4

Key issues in profiling

We have already seen that profiles have frequently been developed in the past as ad hoc solutions to specific problems.

Today, it is important to look at six key issues:

4.1 The formative–summative debate.
4.2 Profiles and the organisation's assessment policy.
4.3 Profiles and the organisation's recording and reporting policy.
4.4 Profiles and the curriculum.
4.5 Profiling and in-service education.
4.6 Computer assisted profiling.

Unless planning for profiling considers these key issues, the profile may become merely a mechanistic tool.

4.1 The formative–summative debate (see also 7.4)

Debate over the main purpose of profiles centres around whether they should be formative, summative, or both.

a. *Formative* – recording, reporting and commenting upon a student's work, personal qualities and social skills (by either pupil, teacher, or both) *as he or she progresses*. It is intended that students should be helped to identify strengths and weaknesses and to develop aspects of their personality, with the principal aim of improving future attainment and development. It is part of the continuing learning process between pupil and teacher.

b. *Summative* – providing an end statement on a student's overall achievement and performance (this may be at the end of a piece of work, a year, or a school career).

a. Formative profiling

It is this formative process which is relatively new, and which has gained increasing prominence in recent years. It involves a new emphasis on counselling and interaction between student and teacher, but it is also potentially the most rewarding in terms of improved relationships between teachers and pupils. Often it is this improvement in relationships which encourages teachers engaged in profiling to persevere.

Teachers have made comments such as: 'I've come to know my tutor group better', and 'John and I have certainly got on better since profiling started.'

The emphasis within formative profiling lies principally in the desire to aid the diagnosis of students' strengths and weaknesses, to improve self-esteem and motivation, and generally to enhance the personal development of the individual.

Whilst it is only comparatively recently that this formative function has gained prominence, it is now seen by many as the most important contribution which profiling has to make. Many of the early pioneers concentrated their efforts on summative profiles; however, where the aims of teachers had been to provide a better, more complete picture of the school leaver (either for the student's own satisfaction or for the consumption of employers), they have gradually become aware of the formative effects of their profiling processes.

In many cases, some of the incidental benefits of formative profiling were soon evident, but in very few cases was there an overt, clearly defined policy identifying the formative *process* as an integral, important part of profiling.

Whilst it may not have been part of their original intention, these early practitioners, recognising the benefits which accrue when profiling is placed at the centre of the learning process, have been amongst the first to accept the argument that profiling can help in diagnostic assessment, in the improvement of future attainment and in the improvement in the quality of interaction between pupil and teacher.

More recent developments, benefiting from these early experiences, show awareness of the formative implications from the outset: it is encouraging that the Secretary of State recognises the importance of the formative elements within profiling, and allocates two of the four 'Purposes of Records of Achievement' to this aspect.[1]

The cumulative effect of these developments has been to legitimise the efforts of those who have long sought to convince colleagues of the benefits in involving the student in assessment, in discussion of progress and in setting individual learning targets.

It remains to be seen whether this explicit identification of the aims of formative, participative learning encourages schools to make profiling and assessment central to the curriculum policy of the school.

b. Summative profiling

Simplified documents offering end statements or summaries of students' work have been in use for years; students, teachers, parents and employers are accustomed to them.

The summative statement is well established and can be readily understood – in profiles, where the aim is accreditation and provision of an aid to selection, the emphasis lies on the summative element. Thus when the priority of school or college is to provide a report for external consumption, then the summative *product* assumes great importance.

A point which is often overlooked is that almost all early profiles (with one

or two exceptions such as the Swindon RPA Scheme)[2] originated from a desire
to improve the summative school-leaving certificate. The aim may have been
to produce a more sophisticated instrument and to give a more rounded picture
of the individual but, nevertheless, it was rooted firmly in the concept of
profiles as summative end statements. There may, occasionally, have been
contributions from the 'victim', but on the whole they were things which
teachers 'did' to pupils.

c. Formative and summative?

This entails a combination of the formative process culminating in a summative
profile certificate.

It is a fairly straightforward task to produce an 'ideal type' of either a
summative or a formative profile. It is far more difficult to combine the two
into one unified system. The underlying philosophies of the two appear to be
difficult to reconcile. On the one hand, formative profiling is concerned with
improving relationships between students and teachers, and is aimed at
increasing self-esteem and self-confidence; it is geared to improving attainment
and enhancing self-development. On the other hand, summative profiles are more
concerned with reporting and passing judgement upon the student. It would,
however, be an abdication of responsibility to students if no attempt is made
to reconcile the two.

Formative profiling, with all its accompanying benefits, enjoys very little
credibility with employers and other users (Chapter 3). Alternatively, a profile
which is solely summative fails to take advantage of the developmental,
educative processes which accompany formative profiling.

It therefore seems clear that if students and teachers are to reap the full
benefits which may be offered by profiles and profiling, there are sound arguments in favour of attempting to marry the formative profiling process to a
summative profile certificate.

4.2 Profiles and the organisation's assessment policy

Profiles are not, in themselves, a method of assessment: they are a means of
recording assessments. If the methods and processes by which these assessments
are arrived at are unsound or inadequate, then the profile will also prove
unsound. Thus profiles are inevitably and inextricably linked to the school's or
college's approach to assessment.

Assessment impinges upon the whole character and life of the school and
the individual student, yet it is an area which is often neglected both in initial
teacher training and in-service training. The advent of profiles highlights the
discrepancy between the importance of assessment and the resources allocated
to its development.

Profiling has forced us all to look much more closely at the field of student assessment: one thing seems certain – to contemplate the introduction of profiles without at the same time implementing a rigorous review of assessment practices within any institution is to invite a muddled and unsatisfactory outcome.

This can only be a brief consideration of some of the main features of assessment, but it is important, before proceeding any further, to establish what is meant by assessment.

A useful definition is offered by Satterly:

> Educational assessment is an omnibus term which includes all the processes and products which describe the nature and extent of children's learning, its degree of correspondence with the aims and objectives of teaching and its relationship with the environments which are designed to facilitate learning. The overall goal is not to stop at description (whether qualitative or quantitative) but to provide information to be used in decision-making.[3]

This last objective can be readily equated with the discussion of formative profiling.

Not all educationists are in favour of assessment in any guise: arguments ranging for and against include the claim that:

i. it offers an objective, fair means of accrediting young people's achievements
ii. it provides a means of checking the effectiveness of teaching and learning
iii. it assists in the maintenance of standards, and in the selection of career opportunities.

Arguments against assessment include the belief that formal assessment is:

i. anti-educational
ii. a straightjacket upon the curriculum
iii. unfair and destructive of young people's self-esteem
iv. time-consuming
v. even in a so-called 'objective' setting, unreliable.

Despite these criticisms, assessment currently absorbs a large proportion of the school year; therefore every effort should be made to identify school policy, to establish a coherent system with which all staff are familiar and to link the assessment policy firmly with the profiling activities within the school. It is often the advent of profiles which prompts schools to look afresh at assessment.

There are three main approaches to assessment, which have particular relevance for those considering the style of profile which would most readily suit their individual institutions (see also 7.9).

i. *Norm-referenced assessment*: a test which is specifically designed to make comparisons among individuals.
ii. *Criterion-referenced assessment*: in which grades are allocated according to predetermined levels of performance without reference to standards reached by other students.
iii. *Ipsative assessment*: in which young people are compared only with their own past performance.

However, an amalgam of two or three of these approaches is frequently used, and the distinction between norm- and criterion-referencing in particular is often blurred.

These three main approaches function as a basis against which to consider alternative techniques of assessment. Garforth offers the following list of possible techniques:

Diagnostic assessment
Published diagnostic tests
Objectively marked tests
Written examinations
Published tests of attainment
Continuous assessment
Informal teacher tests
Structured observation of pupil performance
Student self-assessment
Informal teacher assessment of personal or attitudinal characteristics
Published personality tests
Oral assessment
Listening tests
Conversation tests
Project assessment
Course work essays assessment
Practical work[4]

Many of these techniques are already familiar within schools, but they often occur in a haphazard, uncoordinated manner. If profiles are to be effective, there needs to be planned correlation between assessment procedures and the profiling process. These should relate not only to appropriate techniques, but to such matters as frequency of assessment, agreed methods of assessment, agreed standards of assessment and standardisation of marks.

Teachers enter the profession with the expectation that they will be able to grade and mark students' work, yet without any thorough training in the requisite skills. The introduction of profiling, with its accompanying review of the assessment system, could offer the chance for a collaborative in-service exercise to improve skills in assessment.

In addition to the factors already suggested for discussion, it is helpful if the whole staff, from probationers to the most experienced teachers, examine and evaluate the purposes of their assessments, whether those purposes be: diagnosis, evaluation, the provision of information or selection.

Many early initiatives in profiling arose from internal review of assessment, recording or reporting, which teachers found wanting: these reviews frequently led to a complete reappraisal and restructuring of the system. One Head, for example, was horrified to discover that even within one department there was no specific policy for assessment, with individual staff adopting different approaches to such fundamental issues as frequency of marking, allocation of grades or marks, and feedback to students. It could be that readers might find it helpful to introduce profiles through a similar review of assessment; alternatively, it could be that the introduction of profiles prompts such a review.

Whichever approach is adopted, recognition of the close relationship between assessment and profiles is likely to prove helpful. Finally, the issues of validity and reliability are central to profiling. Validity reflects the extent to which an assessment measures what it sets out to measure.

Reliability refers to the degree of consistency of measurement of results, whether this is consistency between different teachers, between different contexts or different 'test' situations. Many teachers see reliability as a key factor in the acceptability of profiles, but there may well be times when it is desirable to make assessments in areas where reliability cannot be guaranteed (e.g. in personal attributes).

It is clear even from this brief consideration of the field of assessment that an integrated approach to assessment and profiling is critically important for the success of profiles within the school. There is an opportunity for in-service education and staff development during the introduction of profiles to raise staff awareness of the issues surrounding assessment which have been discussed in this section: the result can be advantageous not only in terms of profiles, and in placing assessment at the centre of the learning process, but in the assessment policy of the organisation as a whole.

4.3 Profiles and the organisation's recording and reporting policy

a. Record-keeping
The traditional end of term report is not the sole example of recording and reporting in schools – there are many different records kept on individuals, for a multitude of purposes. These include entry registers (containing details of age, sex, primary school, home address, parental occupation). There may also be records of standardised tests administered either in the primary or secondary school. Some schools keep records of health problems in the staff room. Confidential records are kept on young people in contact with various caring or disciplinary agencies (e.g. Education Welfare Officer, Child Guidance, Educational Psychologist, etc.).

It is also certain that within any one school a number of teachers will have records of students' overall subject attainment, internal examination results, coursework, attitude, behaviour and, in some cases, achievements and experiences beyond the classroom. What is equally certain is that in many organisations such information is not globally collated and made available – it is quite common for teachers to be unaware of either the difficulties or the outstanding achievements of youngsters whom they teach.

One teacher said 'it wasn't until nearly the end of the Fifth year that I learned that Darren, a slow youth near the bottom of the remedial class, was practically a national standard darts player'.

It may well be that students do not wish to divulge all of their personal experiences and activities; nevertheless, there are considerable advantages in a system whereby the multitude of records and pieces of information are accumulated under one umbrella, and are readily available (subject to exclusions on grounds of confidentiality) to students and teachers alike. As much of the work is already taking place, it would seem to be advantageous to both teacher and student if it is all collated into one central system. A live issue associated with recording is that of 'open records', where all records kept upon an individual are to be accessible to the individual (and the parents). This has implications for both traditional record-keeping and profiling.

The benefits of student recording are fully discussed in Chapter 3, but a process whereby recording is carried out systematically, under an 'open' system, and where material recorded is discussed with, and in some cases contributed to, by the individual is not only the doorway to a better recording system, but supports and underpins the whole philosophy of the formative profiling process discussed earlier in this chapter. It is a process which need not confine itself to profiling, but which can result in far-reaching repercussions throughout the school curriculum.

This argument is reinforced by the DES which says: 'so far as the internal processes are concerned, teachers will need to ensure that the recording activity and the discussions with pupils take place on a regular and systematic basis throughout their subsequent time at school'.[5]

b. Reporting

Having advanced the argument in favour of a more systematic, co-ordinated approach to record-keeping within the school, the next step is to ask 'when we have all this information, what are we going to do with it?'.

The first step is to analyse the current use of recorded information. It is a fair assumption that much of it is never used at all. The remainder may be used variously to provide students with a report of their progress; to inform parents of the attainment and performance of their children; to identify students for reallocation of form or set (usually promotion or demotion); to provide a summary of each individual's attainment for Head, Head of House, Head of Year, tutor; to provide the basis of a summative report for youngsters seeking admission to Further or Higher Education; to form the basis for confidential references for employers and, increasingly, for those entering YTS.

The form of existing reports varies widely: the old single sheet, single line report still exists, with space for brief comments, encouraging the lapse into cliché: 'Has made pleasing progress' 'Must try harder' (see Fig. 4.1).

Many reports now adopt the 'cheque book' system, whereby each teacher is allocated a page which is completed independently and finally collated into one document, which helps to obviate the problem of teachers being influenced by the remarks of others.

Even when existing reports are inadequate or unsatisfactory, an enormous

		REPORT		Term _Autumn_ 19 81	

Name _Jane Hitchcock_   Age _12 years 9 months_

Form _4B22_   Average Age of Form _12 years 10 months_

SUBJECT OF STUDY	EXAMINATION STANDARD	GENERAL REMARKS	Initials
English ...		Jane is making very good progress.	J.H.
Religious Education ...			
History ...			
Geography ...		Jane has worked well this term and is making steady progress.	M.D
Latin		Jane works with interest and her progress is pleasing.	Cu.
French ... Set 1		Jane's written work is often good, but she should try to contribute more orally.	AME.
German ...			
Mathematics Set 1		Jane is working well. She is a lively member of the class.	J.C.
Physics ...		Jane works well and with ability but she needs to develop more confidence in her work.	JPW
Chemistry ...			
Biology or Physical Science		Jane is keen and works well.	L.H.A.
Art		Jane has adopted a thoughtful and constructive approach to the subject which has resulted in the production of some very good work.	EE
Craft ...			
Music ...		Jane works steadily and she takes an interest	J.N.R
Cookery ... Needlework		Jane has done some very good work	JB
Dance ...		Jane dances well and always works hard.	J.C
Gym		Jane works hard in lessons. She has shown some good partner work this term	P.J.L

Returned Lessons   Times absent O

General Remarks

_____ Form Mistress

The next term begins on   _J. Hume_ _____ Head Mistress

Fig. 4.1: An example of a single sheet report

amount of time is devoted to them. If an integrated profiling and reporting system, linked to the assessment policy of the school, can be devised, the prospects for improved reports, giving fairer, more detailed and more accurate records, are greatly improved.

Benefits accruing from in-service training in assessment should enhance the quality of report writing, promoting clarity of expression and more detailed explanation which will enable the reader to obtain *real* information.

If a positive policy is adopted towards formative assessment and record-keeping, there can be a logical progression towards formative discussion of reports. Nothing is more frustrating for parents or students than the imposition of judgements by teachers which, in many cases, it is not even possible to discuss or question.

In purely practical terms, the merging of profiling and reporting may offer one answer to the fears about time involved in profiling – it may be that we are looking at a rationalisation of existing time rather than the need for more.

The categories included in most profiles would seem to fit the requirement of employers (see Fig. 2.3, p. 33) far more closely than do existing reports. With the spread of profiles, employers should become more familiar with them, and problems associated with credibility and acceptability should diminish.

An integrated approach to assessment, to recording and to reporting should enable the school report (both internal and external) to become a positive, productive activity with a worthwhile end product.

To summarise:

i. Reporting is done now – it takes considerable time and has no formative spin-off.
ii. Since most profiling is relatively structured, it enjoys improved reliability over traditional reporting.
iii. As students are involved in profiling it has formative uses.
iv. Moreover, profiling may take no more time than existing practices.

In spite of powerful arguments in favour of an integrated system, the imposition of an 'off-the-shelf' model onto an existing unchanged system is *not* the most effective way to approach the reconciliation of profiling and school reports. It is only necessary to look at some of the existing TVEI models to appreciate this fact. This does not mean that schools and colleges should not adopt and adapt existing models – there may eventually be a limited number of profiles operating within national guidelines, and adapted locally. What is important is that any profile, whether developed inside the institution or adapted from outside, should be subject to a rigorous review in order to ensure that there is compatibility between the profile and the organisation's approach to assessment, recording and reporting.

4.4 Profiles and the curriculum

'Profiles will revolutionise the curriculum'. This is a dramatic claim – perhaps it is more accurate to say 'Profiles *could* revolutionise the curriculum.'

Schools which have developed their own profile as a reflection of school or college policy, based upon agreement as to the aims and values of the organisation, have found that the curriculum is enriched and enhanced by the incorporation of profiling. This does not imply that it is impossible to graft on an existing model: it does mean that it is necessary to go through the same process of reviewing aims, objectives and values in order to ensure that there is compatibility between those of the organisation and the proposed profile.

The greatest influence for change is effected by the formal assessment of skills, knowledge, attitudes and qualities which were not previously assessed. By assessing, and thereby recognising as important, qualities such as co-operation with others and initiative, schools, colleges and individual teachers are faced with a requirement to look at the curriculum, and to consider whether what is on offer affords the opportunity for young people to acquire, practise and display such qualities. The formative, interactive nature of profiling calls for a completely different approach to teaching, and to relationships with students; this too, will influence the curriculum.

Assessment of cross-curricular skills calls for a new awareness of the need for co-operative teaching and assessment, breaking down barriers between individual subjects in the interests of developing skills which will better prepare the student for coping in adult life (Chapter 6). In some cases this will require new strategies, though in many, opportunities for the development of these skills already exists. Profiling pinpoints the necessity for drawing together the often disparate strands of the curriculum, developing new approaches and formally recognising a broader, more liberal approach to the curriculum. Barbara Pearce observes that 'the opportunities for learning and developing such skills exist in abundance, the failing is in our ability to recognise and validate them'.[6] This is to a large extent true but there is room for, and indeed should be, an element of revolution.

One proposal for curriculum change is cited in the Hargreaves Report.[7] It is suggested that the curriculum should be restructured into units of six or eight weeks, so that work is focussed on shorter term objectives, with credits given at the end of each unit. This should add meaning to the work undertaken by students – objectives which are attainable in the foreseeable future are set, and a series of credits build up to a profile of assessed achievements. This supports the belief that assessment should be central to the learning process.

The most exciting effect of successful profiling is that it prompts teachers to look afresh at what they are teaching and how they are teaching it. If the evidence of those already active in the field is anything to go by, this will have repercussions on teaching style throughout the school.

Basically, education is assessment led. If we change the way we look at assessment, we need to change our view of the curriculum.

4.5 Profiles and in-service education (see also 2.6)

This is probably the only issue connected with profiling about which there is universal agreement – profiles mean in-service education. The need for new teacher skills in counselling, negotiation, recording and reporting all demand extensive training.

Teachers are naturally reluctant to embark upon an activity which they find unfamiliar and in which they feel unskilled and unconfident. It is pointless debating the revolutionised curriculum if teachers are not equipped to mount the revolution.

The nature and extent of in-service education required varies according to the degree of expertise already existing within an institution. Areas for in-service education can be found within the titles of the sub-headings for this chapter. Before embarking upon profiling, in-service education on some or all of these areas will be needed. That is:

negotiation and counselling (for formative, inter-active profiling)
experiential teaching styles
assessment techniques
record-keeping and reporting techniques
computer assisted profiling.

These needs may be answered either:
i. by the provision of centrally organised courses covering topics of general interest to all profilers, which may include dissemination of information, and general training in the broad categories identified
or by:
ii. the institution of school-based inset, designed to meet the identified needs of the individual institution, and which might include:

groups of teachers working together to establish the aims and underlying value base of profiling within the organisation;
identifying areas to be assessed – both within discrete subjects and in cross-curricular skills;
sharing of experience and expertise;
establishing common policies of recording, reporting and assessment.

Whilst some proportion of inset provision will necessarily be in the form of centralised information-giving, there is no substitute for the lessons learned by practical, participative activities. Barbara Pearce describes two such activities (the clapping game and a skills exercise involving the building of Lego models, laying a table, etc.) which elicit in staff an awareness of the implications of a whole range of facets related to assessment and to interpersonal skills more effectively than any formal presentation could achieve.[8]

The most effective approach to in-service education is probably a combination of formal input and workshop sessions, but certainly the development of inset related directly to the needs of the members of the organisation is essential if there is to be any sense of 'ownership' of profiling, rather than resentment at an irritating imposition.

Before any profile is introduced it is advisable that specific inset needs are identified, and a programme designed to meet those needs established. (Chapter 7 may be helpful in establishing priorities and identifying needs.)

4.6 Computer assisted profiling

a. Introduction
The widespread use of profiling as a means of assessment in YTS, prevocational courses such as CGLI 365 and RSA courses, and the identification of profiling as a central component of CPVE and TVEI has made it inevitable that the use of computers to minimise administration and paperwork should be investigated, both in the post-16 sector, and increasingly throughout the school.

Depending upon the system adopted by the institution, profiling appears at first sight to be an ideal candidate for computerisation. It is not, however, advisable to generalise about either the method to be used, or the value of using computers without carefully considering some of the crucial issues. These include questions such as:

Is the system to operate as part of a data base for all school pupils, with profiles forming only part of the operation?

Is a computerised profile to be developed which applies to one specific course?

Is a comment bank approach to be adopted, with a facility to call up and process statements?

Is the computerised profile to consist of unconnected printed profile statements?

Should a word-processing programme using software be used, or a sophisticated, data base programme involving an integrated word-processor?

These are the questions: the answers will vary from institution to institution.

It is not the intention of this section to offer a comprehensive review of all the computer aided profile initiatives currently under investigation or implementation: rather it is the intention to highlight some of the main advantages and disadvantages, and to refer to a selection of practitioners adopting different approaches to the use of computers, in order to help identify the most appropriate system (if any) for your organisation.

b. Advantages associated with computer assisted profiling
1. *Time saving* This is the argument most frequently advanced by advocates of the computer in profiling. It can be further broken down into elements of time saved by:

i. Teachers: possibility of being able to sit in front of a screen, call up comments and print, offers the shortest route to obtaining a profile.
ii. Teachers: should teachers not wish to use the actual hardware, it is still possible to save time by completing a simple proforma (see Fig. 4.7) which is then processed by clerical or technical staff.
iii. Clerical staff: there need be no clerical requirements for the production of a profile if the direct approach outlined in (i) is adopted.
iv. Administration procedures: the huge amount of paperwork passed to staff for completion is considerably reduced.
v. Speed of production: with a well-organised system it is possible to produce more profiles more quickly at any time than under the old, handwritten system.

It is a good idea if, before imposing any system of computer profiling on teachers in an assumption that time will be saved, staff are consulted about whether in their view the quickest method of producing profiles is to sit and handwrite comments, to complete a standardised proforma or to computerise the process.

2. *Superior product* It is important that young people should receive an impressive, well-finished document. With adequate word-processing facilities it should be possible for all students to receive profiles of pleasing standard appearance.

3. *Information retrieval* There are many reasons why information contributing to the profile may be required before the end of the 5th year – job applications, individuals moving to another area, transfer to another school within the area, etc. With computerisation, the profile with information available to date can be produced at any time.

4. *Information storage* The computer offers a central storage facility which rationalises data, and reduces the proliferation of paper normally surrounding record-keeping.

5. *Student involvement* Students are able to gain hands-on experience with computers if they are able to enter and retrieve information relating to their profile.

c. Disadvantages associated with computer assisted profiles

1. *Staff resistance* One of the biggest drawbacks to the use of computers may be the reluctance of many teachers to sit down in front of a computer, and use it as a tool. It may appear more of a threat than an aid. This, in itself, has massive implications for:

2. *In-service training* This must come first, and has far-reaching consequences in terms of time, money and facilities. It is, however, an essential element in any proposal to introduce computer aided profiles. Patrick Bird highlights this point when he says:

Teachers must be made aware of what the computer can and cannot do. They must realise that computer programs are not infallible, that the computer does not control them or their pupils, and neither can it make judgements. It must be seen merely as a processor of information which is valuable in helping them with their job.[9]

3. *Invasion of privacy* A major concern of many teachers is the 'big brother' association of computers storing information about individuals. Associated with this fear are issues relating to confidentiality of information, invasion of privacy and the ethics of recording and reporting. Some of these worries were addressed in the LAMSAC Report.[10]

In July 1984 the Data Protection Act received the Royal Assent, with the intention that it should come into force in stages over the following three or four years. Registered data users must comply with the following eight data protection principles:

1. The information contained in personal data shall be obtained and the personal data shall be processed fairly and lawfully.
2. The personal data shall be held only for one or more specified and lawful purposes.
3. Personal data held for any purpose or purposes shall not be used or disclosed in any manner incompatible with that purpose or with those purposes.
4. Personal data shall be adequate, relevant and not excessive for the purpose or purposes for which it is held.
5. Personal data shall not be kept longer than is necessary for the specified purpose or purposes.
7. An individual shall be entitled –
   a) at reasonable intervals, and without undue delay or expense –
   i. to be informed by any data user whether he holds personal information of which that individual is the subject; and
   ii. to access to any such data held by a data user; and
   b) where appropriate, to have such data corrected or erased.
8. The data user must take appropriate security measures against unauthorised access to, alteration, disclosure or destruction of personal data and against accidental loss or destruction of personal data.[11]

Information which is kept by traditional, manual means is not subject to this legislation.

4. *Appropriate use of teacher time* Some people may question whether sitting in front of a computer processing student profiles is what teachers *should* be doing. Despite the fact that there may be an overall saving of time, it can be argued that teachers' skills and professional expertise should be exercised in the teaching of students, and should not be diverted into 'peripheral' activities.

5. *Stereotyped profiles* There is a danger that with a limited number of comments upon which to draw, student profiles will become stereotyped, while if the comments are expanded, the process of selecting comments becomes too time-consuming.

6. *Look-alikes*   Associated with the danger of stereotyping is the possibility of students receiving very similar profiles. Once the personalised concept of profiling is removed, the relevance and interest to students is reduced.

7. *Technical limitations*   If the most readily accessible micro-computers are used there are problems associated with storage of information. Even with word-processing facilities, without a powerful, sophisticated machine, limitations are imposed on the amount of data which can be stored on a single floppy disc. For example, using a comment bank approach, a separate file is required for each comment. This means that the large number of files quickly fill a disc, which is clearly undesirable. (There is every sign that new technology in the form of hard discs offers the opportunity for the storage of more information. When the present generation of business micros using hard discs becomes commonplace in schools, this could have beneficial possibilities for their use in profiling.)

8. *Limited flexibility*   Computer assisted profiling can limit flexibility; there is a danger of the computer dictating the shape of the profile rather than simply facilitating procedures.

It seems clear that the potential exists for computers to assist and facilitate the use of profiles in schools. National, local and individual initiatives are pursuing this goal, with varying degrees of success.

It does appear, however, that at the moment software development has not yet reached the stage where the production of profiles from computer stored data is straightforward.

The alternatives discussed in this chapter each have associated strengths and weaknesses: the purpose-built programme relating to a specific course described by FEU has the strength of both requiring the setting of objectives for the course in clear, unambiguous terms available to teachers and students, and of facilitating speedy, readily accessible printouts. The programme is not, however, suitable (nor is it intended) for use throughout the institution for all students on all courses.

A comment bank approach, which may be suitable for all students, requires a comment bank which has been carefully and thoughtfully compiled – it is all too easy to fill the computer up with rubbish if additional comments can be added in an ad hoc fashion. It also calls for a machine which can handle a large, complicated process in order to avoid the problems associated with a proliferation of files. This highlights the issue of the advantages offered by the capacity of a large, sophisticated computer system versus the accessibility of the micro.

Whichever system of computer aided profiling is adopted, there is a need for a word-processing facility which can process comments into meaningful prose, and can format the final profile into an acceptable form.

d. Some examples of computers as aids to profiling
1. Further Education Unit: Computer aided profiling[12]
This paper from FEU is the account of a case study at North Warwickshire

```
┌─────────────────────────────────────────────────────────────────────────────┐
│  STUDENT PROFILE ASSESSMENT            INDEXICES etc.                          │
│                                        Shows good grasp of alphabetical arrange│
│                                        some knowledge of where to begin to look│
│  Course Title: PRE-CARING              1.13    LISTENING                       │
│                                        Listens well inder ideal conditions — ne│
│  Student:                              instructions.                           │
│                                        1.14    PERSONAL ORAL COMMUNICATION     │
│  Date: 07-Jun-82                       Can cope with most one-to-one encounters│
│                                        encouragement to sustain interchange.   │
└─────────────────────────────────────────────────────────────────────────────┘
```

STUDENT PROFILE ASSESSMENT

Course Title: PRE-CARING

Student:

Date: 07-Jun-82

LITERACY

1.01   READING:
Reads fluently without hesitation, and in an intelligent manner, a wide variety of reading material including books, newspapers etc.
1.02   INTERPRETING WRITTEN MATERIAL (PROSE)
Can understand a variety of written material if written in straight-forward manner.
1.03   INTERPRETING DIAGRAMMATIC MATERIAL
Understands most forms of diagrammatic presentations, but unsure about the more complex systems.
1.04   DRAWING DIAGRAMS
Can produce simple sketch maps or diagrams.
1.05   HANDWRITING
Handwriting is clear and easy to read in joined script. Fluent in execution.
1.06   PRESENTATION AND APPEARANCE OF WORK
Work usually shows care in presentation — some room for improvement.
1.07   VOCABULARY
Some attempt at developing range of words used. Fluent but limited.
1.08   GRASP OF CONVENTIONAL LETTER LAYOUTS
Can write an acceptable letter observing most of the conventions of letter layout.
1.09   SIMPLE DESCRIPTIONS
Can describe with help how to perform simple operations.
1.1   SIMPLE FACTUAL REPORTS
Can give in a reasonably ordered fashion an account of straight-forward events. May omit points.
1.11   FORM FILLING
Can cope with most forms in a legible and accurate manner.
1.12   USE OF DIRECTORIES, ALPHABETICAL LISTS,

INDEXICES etc.
Shows good grasp of alphabetical arrangement and has some knowledge of where to begin to look for information.
1.13   LISTENING
Listens well inder ideal conditions — needs reinforcement on instructions.
1.14   PERSONAL ORAL COMMUNICATION
Can cope with most one-to-one encounters. Needs encouragement to sustain interchange.
1.15   GROUP ORAL COMMUNICATION
Will take part if encouraged.
1.16   USE OF TELEPHONE
Can use public and private telephone effectively in most situations.
1.17.   SYNTAX
Writes inaccurately constructed simple sentences. Limited use of relative clauses.
1.18   PUNCTUATION
Can use most punctuations accurately.
1.19   SPELLING
Can spell most words accurately.
1.2   ORGANISATION OF IDEAS
Can organise familiar ideas in coherent fashion.

NUMERACY

2.01   FOUR RULES
Can perform a range of skills — perhaps using a calculator for more difficult examples.
2.02   TABLES
Can utilise most tables up to 12 times with acceptable degree of accuracy.
2.03   PLACE-VALUE
Grasps place value significance in most straight-forward examples.
2.05   FRACTIONS — FOUR RULES
Can cope with very straight-forward calculations. May have difficulty in transferring the principles to situations.
2.07   STANDARD UNITS
Conversant with units — can compare imperial with metric and work with some ease in all modes, read timetables etc. Reasonably accurate in estimating. Measures accurately with variety of instruments.
2.08   RATIO AND PROPORTION
Can deal with more straight-forward relationships eg. scaling up a half to a whole number relationship.

Fig. 4.2: A computer assisted profile

College of Technology and Art, where a computer assisted profile was designed for a pilot scheme involving a full-time vocational course in Caring. Briefly, staff involved in the course devised a series of descriptors showing what students can do (emphasising positive achievement) (see Fig. 4.2). Teachers are required to select codes for appropriate comments, and transfer them to an assessment sheet (Fig. 4.3). The computer then translates these codes into the chosen statements and prints them onto the final profile in the form of profile sentences. In addition to the planning required of staff teaching the course, considerable liaison in design of the system with computer staff is called for.

This is an example of a computer assisted profile designed to fit a specific type of course — which may be easier to implement than a generic approach. Further details can be obtained from:

Further Education Unit, *Computer aided profiling* (occasional paper), 1983.

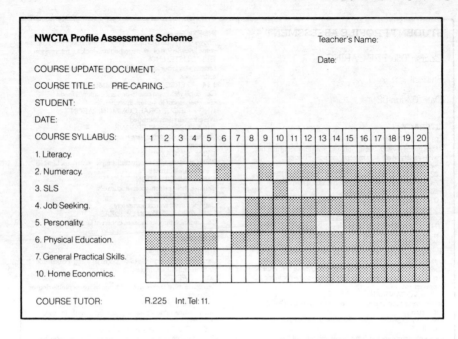

NWCTA Profile Assessment Scheme   Teacher's Name:

                                                        Date:

COURSE UPDATE DOCUMENT.

COURSE TITLE: PRE-CARING.

STUDENT:

DATE:

COURSE SYLLABUS:	1	2	3	4	5	6	7	8	9	10	11	12	13	14	15	16	17	18	19	20
1. Literacy.																				
2. Numeracy.																				
3. SLS																				
4. Job Seeking.																				
5. Personality.																				
6. Physical Education.																				
7. General Practical Skills.																				
10. Home Economics.																				

COURSE TUTOR: R.225   Int. Tel: 11.

NWCTA Profile Assessment Scheme   Teacher's Name:

                                                        Date:

COURSE UPDATE DOCUMENT.

COURSE TITLE: PRE-CARING.

STUDENT: A. N. Other

DATE: May 7th 1982

COURSE SYLLABUS:	1	2	3	4	5	6	7	8	9	10	11	12	13	14	15	16	17	18	19	20
1. Literacy.	1	2	2	3	2	2	2	2	3	3	3	2	2	2	2	2	3	3	2	3
2. Numeracy.	1	1	2		4		1	3		4										
3. SLS	2	2	3	3	3	3	2	4	3		N/A	3	3	3						
4. Job Seeking.	2	2	2	3	2	2	2													
5. Personality.	2	2	2	1	1	1	1				1	2								
6. Physical Education.					2															
7. General Practical Skills.	2				2	2	1	2												
10. Home Economics.	1	2	2	1	2	2	2	3	2	2	3	2								

COURSE TUTOR: R.225   Int. Tel: 11.

Fig. 4.3: Assessment sheet for the computer assisted profile shown in Fig. 4.2

2. Individual school profile

An example of a school which has devised its own computer assisted profile can be found in The Vineyard Observation and Assessment Unit, Telford. Edward Carron has written a development programme in BASIC which will relate to the needs of pupils in his own school for socially handicapped pupils.

It differs from the previous example in that this programme is designed to provide a data base on all pupils, and the profile forms only a small part of that data base.

Its programme also differs in that it uses BASIC language, which has the disadvantage of producing a profile which is not formated – words tend to run on from one line to the next. This is a technical problem which most programmers can readily overcome. This system does, however, solve the problem of making sufficient information available without filling discs with a multitude of files. Further information can be obtained from:

Mr Edward Carron, The Vineyard Observation and Assessment Unit, Vineyard Road, Wellington, Telford.

3. TVEI Profile Project 1984

The London Borough of Havering, which has enjoyed a leading role in educational computing (including development of JIIG – CAL and diagnostic learning profiles), is engaged upon a pilot scheme for the development of student profiles under the TVEI, based upon its three existing software programmes for

i. using diagnostic curriculum testing for formative and summative evaluation
ii. JIIG – CAL (Job Information and Ideas Generator – Computed Assisted Learning) Careers Education and Guidance to build up reports of students' career potential (see 2.5)
iii. hierarchical database system (Image II) with an equally sophisticated enquiry language which exists on the Educational Computer Centre's Hewlett Packard (HP) system.[13]

The proposal for research identifies the problems raised by rapid technological development, and aims to develop as flexible (and transportable) a system as possible.

This is an example of a wider ranging project to develop computer aided profiles, on the part of an organisation which already has considerable experience of using computers in educational learning and reporting. Further information can be obtained from:

Mr W.R. Broderick, London Borough of Havering, Educational Computer Centre, Tring Gardens, Harold Hill Romford RM3 9QX.

4. School-based profile linked to County initiative – two alternative approaches

1. The original computer assisted profiling implemented by Phil Neal at Lea Manor High School and Community College used a comment bank approach with a Wordstar word-processing package together with Mail merge on a 380 Z micro.

Up to 128 comments per department were available. In general, departments chose to have five sections within the final report, with each section used to comment on a different area of the subject. As most departments used approximately sixty to seventy comments, this provided adequate capacity. The word processor was able to format and print the selected comments onto separate report slips which were then collated by the tutor.

This is the stage towards which many schools are currently working. However, Lea Manor have now refined and developed the process further.

2. The Mark II version of the computer assisted profile takes advantage of the fact that the school is participating in the Bedfordshire project looking at computerisation of school administration.

This uses the Sirius micro-computer, and the d Base II software. There is virtually no upper limit to the number of comments which can be held on disc, and the reports can be collated and printed onto A4 paper. An additional five sections (ten in all) are available, but in practice most departments still use five. The system is being operated in Bedfordshire TVEI schools.

The summative profile consists of

examination results
tutor's assessment of interests, experience of work and personal qualities
student's own assessment of interests, experiences of work and personal
   qualities
summary of skills and abilities of the student.

A comment bank approach is again adopted – an example of comment bank (see Fig. 4.4) and final output (see Fig. 4.5) is provided for both subject assessment (physics) and cross-curricular skills (listening and talking) (see Fig. 4.6). Staff select the appropriate phase and enter the code number on a data collection sheet (see Fig. 4.7). This is translated, formated and printed by the micro.

Detailed explanations are available including instructions for printing, editing, re-ordering teaching groups; adding, amending or deleting comments; changing, adding or removing headings; and printing comments.

This is clearly a fairly sophisticated computer assisted profiling system, which has resulted from constant review and revision, and which will doubtless be modified still further in the future. It does give a realistic idea of what can be achieved by using the computer to facilitate profiling.

Requirements:
Computer able to run d Base II
d Base II (registered trade mark of Ashton Tate)
Bedfordshire School Administration System
d Base II Profiling/Reporting System
Quad Density 5.25″ Floppy Discs, 12″ × 9.25″ 2 Sheet NCR Paper,
12″ × 9.25″ Paper, 14″ × 11″ Music ruled paper

Further information from: Phil Neal, Lea Manor High School and Community College, Northwell Drive, Luton LU3 3TL.

```
        Physics as Year 4 Reports        12/11/84
```

A1
Jenny is an extremely able pupil who has worked hard to understand Physics.

A2
Jenny is an able pupil who has worked hard to understand the subject.

A3
Although Jenny has not found Physics easy to understand, she has worked hard and has made progress.

A4
Although Jenny has found the subject difficult to get to grips with, she has worked hard to overcome her problems of understanding.

A5
Jenny is an able pupil but her slightly immature attitude to formal study means that unless she is constantly supervised, she will not work to her full potential.

A6
Jenny finds Physics difficult to understand but this is partly due to her immature approach to study and her tendency not to concentrate in the lesson.

A7
Jenny appears to take an interest in this subject but, at times, she fails to concentrate fully in class.

A8
Jenny works competently and well in Physics and shows an interest in the subject.

A9
Jenny has ability but needs to put more effort into her work in order to reach her full potential in this subject.

A10
Jenny does not find this subject particularly easy to understand, but with a more determined effort could make better progress.

A11
Jenny finds this subject difficult to understand and must make a determined effort in order to overcome her difficulties.

A12
Jenny is an able pupil who always puts a great deal of effort into her work and is developing a sound understanding of the subject.

A13
Jenny has ability and shows interest in this subject although she does not always work to her full potential.

Fig. 4.4: Part of a comment bank for the computer assisted profile

Physics Year 4 Reports   12/11/84

B1
Her written work is very neatly presented, accurate and detailed.

B2
Her written work is neatly presented, accurate and fairly detailed.

B3
Her written work is fairly neat and contains a reasonable amount of detail.

B4
Her work is rather untidy and lacks important detail.

B5
Her written work is slightly untidy but reasonably detailed.

B6
Her written work lacks detail and assignments are often incomplete.

B7
She tends to rush her work and consequently her work lacks detail on occasions.

B8
Her written work is neatly presented but lacks detail.

B9
Her written work reveals understanding of the concepts involved but it is not always
completed satisfactorily.

B10
Her written work is neatly presented but sometimes reveals only superficial
understanding of the concepts involved.

Physics Year 4 Reports   12/11/84

C1
Whilst her experimental investigations are well thought through and reported.

C2
Whilst her experimental investigations are carried out well.

C3
Whilst her experimental investigations are quite well reported.

C4
Whilst her experimental investigations are carried out correctly but not always
fully understood.

C5
Whilst her experimental work is carried out quite well but is not reported in
sufficient detail.

C6
Whilst a more determined effort is required during practical sessions in order to
obtain reliable results from experiments.

C7
Whilst her approach to experimental assignments is confident.

C8
Whilst her experimental investigations are carried out sensibly and results are
recorded carefully.

C9
Whilst she sometimes lacks confidence when undertaking experimental investigations.

Fig. 4.4 (cont.)

```
            Physics Year 4 Reports              12/11/84
   D1
   Her lively, outgoing personality allows Jenny to talk freely in class
   discussions and ask questions when she does not grasp an idea.

   D2
   Her outgoing personality allows Jenny to talk freely in class discussions but
   she has a tendency to be slightly over-confident in her arguments.

   D3
   She has a tendency to remain silent in class discussions and does not ask for help
   even when it is needed.

   D4
   She is rather quiet in class discussions avoiding the limelight as often as possible.
   Her knowledge of the subject could be increased if she was prepared to ask
   questions.

   D5
   Although she is quiet in class discussions, she is not afraid to ask questions if it
   is necessary.

   D6
   Jenny only occasionally participates in class discussions and does not ask for
   help as often as she should do.

   D7
   Jenny participates willingly in class discussions, revealing a sound grasp of the
   principles of Physics.

   D8
   Jenny should try to take a more active part in class discussions since this would
   help her to increase her understanding of the principles of Physics.

   D9
   Jenny must try to overcome her reluctance to ask for help in class if she is to
   increase her understanding of the principles of Physics.

   D10
   Jenny participates in class discussions but would benefit from making more
   frequent contributions.

   D11
   Jenny participates willingly in class discussions.

   D12
   Clearly, a more mature attitude towards study is required if Jenny is to reach
   her full potential in this subject.
```

```
┌─────────────────────────────────────────────────────────────────────────┐
│ John WILLIAMS              Tutor Group:  4G      November 1984             │
│                                                                           │
│ Subject        Level         Comment                                      │
│ ─────────────────────────────────────────────────────────────────────── │
│ French         Upper         John is a most conscientious pupil who always puts│
│                Intermediate  a great deal of effort into his work.  He is making│
│                              steady progress in his written work.  Orally, he is│
│                              confident and competently displays his spoken skills.│
│                              He has therefore achieved a sound test result.│
│                                                                           │
│                                                                           │
│                                          .......................          │
│                                          M. Webb                          │
│                                                                           │
│ History        High          John is a very able pupil with a mature and sensible│
│                              approach towards his studies.  He displays a sound│
│                              grasp of the factual content of the course but has│
│                              experienced some difficulties in handling items│
│                              involving the use of historical evidence.  John has│
│                              displayed his ability and confidence to good effect│
│                              in many classroom discussions.  His examination mark│
│                              is very good reflecting a sound approach to revision│
│                              and a high potential in any external examination│
│                              entry.                                        │
│                                                                           │
│                                          .......................          │
│                                          P. Smith                         │
│                                                                           │
│ English        Upper         John has worked extremely hard this year, displaying│
│                Intermediate  a positive attitude towards English lessons.  He has│
│                              attained a high standard of general accuracy and his│
│                              written style is lively and imaginative.  He should│
│                              continue to extend his vocabulary through reading│
│                              widely.  His response to literature is perceptive and│
│                              thoughtful, although his coursework does not always│
│                              reflect his true potential.  He is an articulate│
│                              conversationalist and can present and sustain an│
│                              argument particularly well.                   │
│                                                                           │
│                                          .......................          │
│                                          J. Enos                          │
│                                                                           │
│ Mathematics    High          John shows outstanding ability in this subject and│
│                              produces work of the highest standard.  He is a│
│                              conscientious pupil who shows great enthusiasm at all│
│                              times.  John has mastered many of the techniques│
│                              necessary for success in this subject but should pay│
│                              particular attention to problems involving accounts.│
│                              He has sound understanding of basic numeracy and is│
│                              able to calculate effectively both mentally and on│
│                              paper.  If he continues in this way, he should be│
│                              successful in the external examinations next year.│
│                                                                           │
│                                          .......................          │
│                                          A. Brown                         │
└─────────────────────────────────────────────────────────────────────────┘
```

Fig. 4.5: The final output for subject assessment for the computer assisted profile

John WILLIAMS		Tutor Group: 4G November 1984
Subject	Level	Comment
Art	Upper Intermediate	John has worked extremely well at all aspects of this subject and this reflected in his excellent examination result. He obviously has considerable ability which he has fully exploited, and he has handled the materials competently and skilfully to produce some outstanding artwork. His ideas are highly imaginative and always thoughtfully planned out. .... S. Neal
Biology	High	John is an able pupil who works quietly and conscientiously in class. His written work is of a high standard and is always neatly presented, whilst his approach to practical topics reflects his under-standing of the underlying theory. His readiness to answer questions during class discussions indicates a good understanding of Biological principles. .... T. Hitchcock
Physics	Upper Intermediate	Although John has not found Physics easy to understand, he has worked hard and has made progress. His written work is neatly presented, accurate and fairly detailed, whilst his experimental investigations are carried out well. His outgoing personality allows John to talk freely in class discussions but he has a tendency to be slightly over-confident in his arguments. .... P. Neal
Drama	Upper Intermediate	John is always an enthusiastic and an interested member of the group. He involves himself fully in Drama both within and beyond the classroom. His oral work is inventive and exciting and is developed to a high standard in a variety of roles and characteris-ations. He revels a real desire to achieve the best. His folder is a full and detailed one with vivid and perceptive reports on his practical work. There is good evidence to show that he has the ability to criticise his own practical work. John is a lively member of the schools's Manor Youth Theatre. He has been fully involved in this year's productions. .... D. Wood

Karen WALLIS		Registration Group : A　November 1984
Communications	Listening & Talking	Karen is confident considerate and mature in conversations with both peers and adults. She reponds positively to suggestions and can follow complex instructions. In both formal and informal discussions she shows a strong grasp of subject matter and specialist vocabulary and she is able to contribute in an appropriate manner in a variety of situations.
	Reading and Understanding	Karen has shown a high level of understanding of the different styles of written and visual material. She can read simple written material and extract information from it with guidance.
	Writing	Karen uses mature judgement and an extensive vocabulary to tackle a wide variety of written tasks, both familiar and new, suiting style and form to the situation. She spells and punctuates well using both simple and complex sentences.
Mathematical Skills	Numeracy	Karen is very competent in all aspects of numeracy and is able to select and apply appropriate methods to solve multi-step problems with a high degree of sucess. She make excellent use of a calculator when necessary and calculates mentally with speed and accuracy.
Practical	Dexterity & Co-ordination	Karen can manipulate things reasonably. If you ask her to do something calling for simple dexterity and co-ordination it will take her some time and effort. More complex tasks she could manage with some support from staff, and when faced with a task needing great manipulation, control and accuracy she can work towards a high standard.
	Using Equipment	Having been given instruction on basic equipment Karen can perform simple tasks safely with some guidance. She has been able to use more specialised items of equipment with minimal supervision. Faced with a new situation, Karen will select the correct equipment and material with reasonable success and without any significant help. She is able to select and operate equipment in order to perform more advanced tasks after some consultation.
Information Retrieval		Karen is able to recognise when she needs information and will make resonable attempts to explain what she wants. She is familiar with a wide range of reference books and other resources including computer databases and has experience of using maps, timetables, directories and detailed indexes. Faced with a mass of information, she can usually select what is relevant unaided.
Problem Solving and Planning		Karen can confidently cope with a wide range of problem-solving exercises and can plan, carry out and evaluate a complex project using a wide variety of resources.
Graphical Awareness		Karen can use and construct complex mathematical charts and graphs with guidance.

Fig. 4.6: The final output for cross-curricular skills for the computer assisted profile

Adro	Name	Reg	Level A	B	C	D	E
2646	ADAM, Paul	C	: 0	: 8	: 5	: 2 :	:
2661	BINNING, Kashmir	M	:	: 2	: 2	: 2 :	:
2658	BOWDEN, Keith	H	:	: 1	: 1	: 1 :	:
2671	CHANDLER, Ian	D	:	: 3	: 5	: 2 :	:
2827	CUMMINE, Karen	H	:	: 1	: 2	: 1 :	:
2832	DEVINE, Denise	E	:	: 3	: 5	: 2 :	:
2693	EVANS, Barry	I	:	: 3	: 3	: 1 :	:
2721	GRACE, Simon	I	:	: 2	: 2	: 2 :	:
2852	HENMAN, Kirsty	C	:	: 3	: 5	: 2 :	:
2955	HOPWELL, Darren	I	:	: 2	: 3	: 3 :	:
2722	JAMES, Jonathon	H	:	: 1	: 1	: 2 :	:
2865	KEEBLE, Sharon	D	:	: 2	: 4	: 2 :	:
3538	LITTLE, Rachel	D	:	: 1	: 1	: 2 :	:
2873	McCANN, Michelle	A	:	: 2	: 3	: 2 :	:
2749	MELLOR, James	B	:	: 1	: 1	: 1 :	:
2881	MULLINS, Sharron	A	:	: 3	: 5	: 2 :	:
2885	PAREKH, Sobhna	S	:	: 2	: 5	: 2 :	:
2890	PITCHFORD, Karen	L	:	: 1	: 1	: 1 :	:
2984	RAINE, Joanne	C	:	: 3	: 5	: 1 :	:
2905	SMITH, Tracy	B	:	: 2	: 3	: 2 :	:
2912	THOMAS, Margaret	E	:	: 3	: 5	: 2 :	:
2795	TYRRELL, Steven	S	:	: 2	: 1	: 2 :	:
2805	WILLIAMSON, Jason	M	:	: 3	: 3	: 2 :	:

Fig. 4.7: A data collection sheet for the computer assisted profile

Summary

This chapter has addressed some of the key issues which are central to the introduction of profiles.

The dilemma of the formative versus summative functions of profiling is considered, and the recommendation is offered that both are of so great an importance that every effort should be made to incorporate a formative, developmental profiling process, with a final summative profile certificate.

The assessment policy of the organisation has major implications in any system of recording assessment. A brief guide to alternative approaches to assessment is outlined; recording and reporting information about students is also central to any consideration of profiling. It seems advisable that any move to introduce profiles should be preceded, or accompanied, by a review of assessment, recording and reporting, in order that a cohesive and compatible policy can be adopted.

The implications for the curriculum are significant. In order to assess a wide range of skills, attributes and qualities not previously formally considered, schools and colleges need to provide opportunities for their acquisition and practice. This may well lead teachers to question what they teach, and how they teach it, and add a new and exciting dimension to the examination-dominated curriculum.

In-service education is one area which it is possible to state firmly is necessary for the successful introduction of profiling. There is a need for support and training in all of the categories discussed in this summary – without adequate inset it is unrealistic to expect teachers to embrace profiling.

The final key issue – computer assisted profiling – is one which is not absolutely essential to the success of any project. It is perfectly possible to introduce profiles without computers. It is still too early to come to any firm conclusion, but it seems likely that although much of the existing software is not sufficiently advanced to fulfil all the requirements of widespread profiling, there are indications that computers offer a way of producing more profiles more quickly, without usurping any of the teachers' expertise or invading the personal interaction essential to any profiling process.

Notes

1. Department of Education and Science, and Welsh Office, *Records of achievement: a statement of policy*, 1984.
2. Curriculum Study and Development Centre, Wiltshire, *The record of personal achievement: tutors' handbook*, Council Education Department, 1974.
3. Satterly, D. *Assessment in schools*, Basil Blackwell, 1981.
4. Garforth, D., *Profile assessment: recording student progress*, Dorset County Council, 1983.
5. Department of Education and Science, and Welsh Office, *Records of achievement*.
6. Pearce, B., Developing the profilers, in Further Education Unit, *Profiles in action*, 1984.
7. Inner London Education Authority, *Improving secondary schools* (The Hargreaves Report), 1984.
8. Pearce, B., Developing the profilers.
9. Bird, Patrick, *Microcomputers in school administration*, Macmillan, 1984.
10. Local Authority Management Services and Computer Committee, *Towards a computer based education management information system*, 1974.
11. Data Protection Act, 1984.
12. Further Education Unit, *Computer aided profiling* (occasional paper), 1983.
13. London Borough of Havering, *TVEI profile project proposal*, unpublished, 1984.

Chapter 5

Pitfalls

Powerful arguments in favour of pupil profiles have been advanced under the umbrella of 'purposes' (Chapter 2). It would be naive, however, to pretend that profiles are not also beset by a number of problems or 'pitfalls'. Some of these pitfalls are widely recognised, and have been the object of varying degrees of concern amongst teachers for some time. Others are less obvious: factors such as surveillance and profiles as agents of social control (5.2) may be less familiar, but are no less important than concerns about, for example, teacher time.

Some of the issues which embody the concerns surrounding profiles include:

5.1 The attempt to be 'all things to all men'.
5.2 Surveillance and social control.
5.3 Subjectivity.
5.4 Untrained or uncommitted staff.
5.5 Time.
5.6 Credibility.
5.7 Ownership.

5.1 The attempt to be 'all things to all men'

One of the pits into which profiles might fall is that of trying to do too many things, of attempting to satisfy the competing claims made upon them, some of which conflict with others, so that the result is a 'mish-mash' of contradictory aims, techniques and outcomes.

This is a pitfall which has been widely recognised, and for which a number of solutions have been sought: the danger is that the proffered solutions may not be sufficient to solve the dilemma. It may be that some of the dilemmas are, in the last analysis, irreconcilable, in which case it is essential that central aims should be identified and prioritised – it is confusion in the aims of profiles and profilers which leads to a woolly attempt to see profiles as a magic panacea which can be 'all things to all men'.

Some of the principal conflicting aims encompassed in this category include:

a. Vehicles for self-development or aids to selection?
There have been two distinct strands detectable in the development of profiles:

first, the student-centred process, with the objective of enhancing self-esteem, self-confidence and encouraging a sense of achievement in the individual. Many of the advocates of this approach have been comparatively uninterested in the response of employers and other users; and secondly, some profiles have developed out of liaison with employers, and the attempt to provide more detailed information in order to aid selection.

The two aims are superficially irreconcilable; I originally subscribed to this view, but I am now convinced that if we are not to abdicate our responsibility for students, some way must be found, not only to give emphasis to the all-important formative process, but also to satisfy the need for certification in a summative statement.

b. Benefiting the school or employers?

This dilemma is similar to the previous category, but differs from it in that it is more concerned with implications for the whole school.

At opposite ends of the spectrum are those who argue for profiles as tools for revolutionising the curriculum, evolving better methods of recording and reporting, improving communications and relationships; whilst at the other there are those who advocate the use of profiles in order to assist employers in their task of sifting and sorting prior to selection.

This highlights the divergence between liberal, educational aims and selection, control procedures.

c. Confidentiality or improved reporting?

One of the overt aims of formative profiling is that a breakthrough should be achieved, involving the liberation of the curriculum and leading to an increased level of communication, negotiation and exchange of information. The degree of confidentiality implicit in the encouragement of students to reveal their innermost thoughts, aspirations and feelings is directly opposed to the concept of improved reporting. Improved reporting calls for the communication of fuller, more detailed information to users.

d. A snapshot-in-time, or an intervention strategy?

The phrase 'a snapshot-in-time' is frequently used in conjunction with profiles.[1] The intention is to signify that the profile is a picture of the young person at one particular stage of development, and is not predictive of future behaviour, attitudes or attainment.

A well-constructed profile, which is the outcome of careful development and a truly formative process offers more than a flat snapshot: it is more akin to a '3D' picture of the individual.

The problem is – is it really only a picture, however detailed, or is it not more accurately described as an intervention strategy? The act of profiling can actually affect and alter the life of the organisation, the behaviour of teachers, and the conduct and reactions of students. Indeed, it is implicit within many of the purposes of profiling that dynamic change will be instigated.

There is a distinct difference between profiles viewed as a better method of offering information about the individual, and profiles as a tool for effecting change.

e. Agreed, negotiated assessment or external criteria?

Early profiles (e.g. FEU, SCRE) were based upon a system involving some degree of norm-referencing, whereby students were allocated to specific bands of attainment in each category assessed. In the case of SCRE each of the bands approximated to 25% of the ability range. Thus in many profiles students are assessed in relation to a norm, or in other cases, in relation to predetermined criteria.

The movement currently gaining strength supports profiles which are based upon a negotiated consensus designed to foster the self-development of individuals, to enable them to set learning targets, and to take an active part in assessing their own performance.

The issues surrounding this pitfall are obscure: any attempt to reconcile a profile which is overtly norm-referenced with a formative, interactive profiling process is likely to experience great difficulty.

f. Profiles for all – or are some less equal than others?

The answer which is rapidly gaining currency is 'profiles must be for all'. This is a relatively new development. Many original profiles were aimed at the less able, and Sir Keith Joseph's original pronouncements foresaw profiles as being aimed at the bottom 40% of the ability range. It is interesting that the latest pronouncement from the DES advocates profiles for all ages and all abilities.[2]

The laudable intention of those advocating universal profiles is that they should not be divisive, and should enjoy a high status which would be impossible if they were seen as only relevant to the less academically successful.

Difficulties arise when attempts are made to cater for students of widely differing attainments, maturity, interests and abilities. Many early profiles experienced difficulties on these grounds, although it is possible to argue that by adopting a negotiated approach and setting individual targets, this problem may be overcome.

Another problem which is thrown up by the inclusion of the whole population in the profiling process is the conflicting interests which may arise between those committed to the promotion of academic subjects, and those who see the pastoral and personal development aspects of the students' schooling as paramount. It would certainly be wrong to prejudice the opportunities of the minority for whom academic excellence is an appropriate and desirable goal. The dilemma revolves around the question 'To what extent is it possible to devise a process and a mechanism equally suitable for *all* students?'.

The danger may well be exacerbated by the fact that teachers, however surrounding the introduction of profiles, all of which may be perfectly legitimate. The basic difficulty lies in trying to make profiles 'all things to all men'.

It may be that awareness of the conflicting values and interests will help to minimise the resulting problems. Compromise may be the best that can be achieved, but compromise should not result in a fudged, confused end product with teachers, students and users all striving to achieve different ends.

5.2   Surveillance and social control

One of the most serious problems posed by the proliferation of profiles is, as yet, largely unrecognised. It is the unacceptable face of assessment – including the whole inter-related area of the use of profiles as agents of social control; of surveillance; of intrusion of privacy; and of the unjustified exposure of the individual. There is a considerable risk that profiles, far from fulfilling the benevolent intentions of enthusiastic protagonists, may in fact prove to be an intrusive, powerful influence reinforcing established social and hierarchical structures within society, and involving the distribution of life-chances across whole sections of society.[3]

This is certainly not the intention of practising teachers, and it is doubtful whether it is the conscious intention of anyone advocating the introduction of profiles.

To understand the real nature of the 'Catch 22' situation in which teachers find themselves, we must go back to the tug of war which has existed within education since the introduction of first external examinations in the early nineteenth century designed to restrict entry to the professions, in ensuring that only those who had demonstrated a certain level of competence should be admitted, and also that the favoured minority who achieved entry to 'the club' enjoyed the enhanced status of exclusivity. On the one hand the role of education and assessment is to provide the liberating effect of offering enlightenment and the opportunity of social mobility to those who could demonstrate the necessary academic and intellectual abilities. On the other hand is the role of assessment as a selective screening tool, and as a method of exercising control. This conflict is often unappreciated by teachers. In a discussion between teachers and a visiting lecturer, it was suggested that a large part of a teacher's function includes the selection, screening and the allocation of life-chances. The overwhelming consensus among teachers present was that teachers' duties were allied solely to the educational aims of producing broader, more autonomous human beings. This is the aspect of teachers' work which provides the rewards and motivates good teachers. The extent to which the categorising of students and participation in 'guidance' towards the most 'appropriate' role in life is part of the teachers' work is frequently unrecognised.

This duality of role for teachers, both in assessment and in education generally, is a recurring cause of conflict – it is not easy to resolve, but it is important to keep it at the forefront of any debate on the value of new forms of recording assessment.

The nature of the control exercised in assessment is two-fold: it exercises control over the individual by its power to affect selection to the meritocracy, and also forms the basis for allowing the government, through establishment-dominated Universities in particular, to retain control of the school curriculum to a very large degree.

Examination syllabuses exert a powerful influence upon what actually happens in school: it may have a constricting and deleterious effect, but it indubitably offers the mechanism for a large degree of state control. This corporate control is one of the phenomena which profile pioneers have sought to resist by offering an alternative approach to assessment. It is certainly evident that the move towards profiles emanates from classroom teachers and is motivated by humanitarian educational concerns. There may, however, be a hint that the government, aware of the strength of feeling throughout education, have stepped in to issue the 1984 Statement of Policy not only as a fairer way of assessing young people, but also in order to re-establish, by the publication of detailed criteria to be observed in profile development, a degree of control by spelling out curricular objectives. This is certainly the view of some members of the teaching profession. It may be too cynical a view, but it is one of which it is as well to be aware. Particularly worrying could be the extent to which a degree of 'social engineering' is facilitated – that is, the restriction of social mobility and the reinforcement of students' views of their place in life.

This last is the aspect of social control which carries the gravest danger in the widespread adoption of profiles. Stronach summarises the position when he states: 'Assessment is not just about knowledge. It is about power as well.'[4]

One of the aims of those responsible for developing profiles is that a number of teachers should be involved in the assessment of individual pupils in order that a fairer, more balanced and fuller picture of the individual should be produced. The often unrecognised corollary to this is that the student has no redress in the event of the final profile proving less complimentary than hoped for.

Despite the notional involvement of the pupil in negotiation and recording procedures, if the document is the result of consensus opinion (even including the student's own) it is more damning as a result of being ostensibly objective. The traditional confidential reference, while frequently unfair and subject to bias, was nevertheless only the result of one person's opinion. The remark 'this reference says more about the person who wrote it than the applicant' is frequently heard. The youngster with a less than brilliant report or reference could always take comfort from the thought 'well, he always had a down on me, I never thought much of him anyway'. The profile offers no such refuge – the student is powerless to resist the power of a benevolent consensus (although in discussion with young people, they seemed unaware of this danger).

The danger may well be exacerbated by the fact that teachers, however unwittingly, are subject to bias, both on the basis of subjective response to individuals' personality, and on the basis of class.[5] In addition to this factor, the students may well object to the degree of exposure of their own person-alities, interests and feelings which are demanded by a profile system. Some students actually object, and state 'it's none of your business!'; however these seem to be in a minority. In most cases young people (and teachers too) are unaware of the potentially insidious nature of intrusive excavation of their personality. The intention is almost always benign, but as Stronach intimates: 'It offers increasingly detailed pictures of pupils to increasingly anonymous administrators. It is bureaucratic knowing, as opposed to personal knowing. In most cases it offers pupils the prospect of being known, but not of knowing.'[6].

This is a potent statement – it has cautionary undertones for those who are unquestioning in their enthusiasm for profiles. That is not to say, however, that it should be accepted unchallenged – it is a basic premise in many of the newer profile systems (viz., Avon, Burgess and Adams) that there should be a real *exchange* between pupil and teacher, necessitating a relationship which is not that of judge and judged.

The danger in this aspect of social control lies in the fact that the individual is exposed to a degree not previously encountered; that the observation and assessment of personal qualities and attitudes crosses the boundary of areas which may be justifiably assessed and is more accurately described as 'surveil-lance'. This has dangerous implications – it conjures up the image of Orwell's '1984' with startling clarity. The qualities and attitudes being assessed become aims in themselves (we value what we assess) and the danger of valuing only those who display the requisite traits will become, however unintentionally, as damaging, or even more so, than the current preoccupation with valuing the academic elite.

5.3 Subjectivity

The danger of damaging students by inflicting the possibly biased, and almost certainly subjective, judgements of teachers upon them, is something which is of major concern to teachers and educational writers alike.

Problems associated with over-exposure and invasion of privacy have already been discussed. These problems are exacerbated by the inevitable introduction of subjectivity.

Does this mean that profiles should eschew all elements calling for comment upon personal qualities? My view is that students are already subject to such assessments, either overt or covert, which are made without any real conscious-ness of their damning nature. The 'he's a pain in the neck' type of comment, which may be translated into more diplomatic language for the report form, is fairly common.

If, then, teachers are already making such statements, it is possible to argue that they should be as professional, open and objective as possible. Teachers are, after all, meant to be professionals: they should surely be trusted to portray, with the increased skills arising from inset, areas which can greatly enhance both the picture of the individual and important qualities which might otherwise pass unrecognised.

This is not to minimise or under-estimate the undoubted dangers inherent in subjectivity. It is merely an attempt to point out that there is no such thing as truly 'objective' assessment. Even the hallowed 'O' level suffers from some degree of subjectivity and bias, both in the content, terminology and language of many of the papers.

Some of the dangers associated with subjectivity include:

a. Bias
The obvious result of a subjective judgement is that it is biased – perhaps with a judgement skewed in favour of the teacher's own views of life whatever they may be.

b. Value laden judgements
It is almost impossible to achieve a value free approach to assessment of students. Teachers are human beings, subject to human weakness; often the value laden nature of the basis for judgements is completely unrecognised. One teacher referring to a group of fourth years said: 'they're like a nest of rats'. It is almost certain that he was quite unaware of the value laden assumptions underlying that remark. It is not easy to rid ourselves of value laden interpret-ations. It *is* possible to be aware of the dangers, to make every effort to counter them, and to try to design assessment instruments which alleviate the worst problems. To begin with, teachers have to make their own values *explicit*. Comments on youngsters' qualities and skills should, as far as possible, be couched in terms of positive achievement, certainly in the summative form (although it has already been stated that negative feedback has a valuable part to play in the formative process).

c. Personality clash
This is a common, and difficult, problem. One teacher who was concerned said: 'I have tried every way to get through to Dawn, but she just doesn't like me, and to be honest, I don't really like her either. How can she receive a fair assessment in those circumstances?'

Many teachers would find it difficult to match that degree of honesty. One solution is that, within a department, another teacher should undertake her profiling. Another safeguard can be the involvement of a number of teachers in each student's profile (an approach which lies at the heart of profiling).

The argument against profiles is that they enable unconscious prejudices to assume a greater importance than would be possible if assessment was confined to the cognitive (although even this is doubtful; 'She had more mistakes than me and she still got a higher mark' is not an uncommon cry).

d. 'Halo' effect

One of the dangers accompanying subjective assessment is the 'halo' effect, whereby teachers who see a student shining or failing in their own particular area of interest, allow that to spill over into other areas of the youngsters' activities – 'Oh, John's a good lad' or 'She's not much good at anything.' It is essential that students should be judged on their actual attributes rather than on perceptions distorted by the 'halo'.

Much of the solution lies in careful, clear definitions, with carefully delineated parameters of what is being assessed, carefully defined language, and in defining the evidence upon which assessments are based.

It is a question of establishing priorities; the need of those whose greatest strengths lie in the area beyond the cognitive domain may well justify the risks to which students may be exposed by teacher subjectivity.

This need is illustrated by one youth who, in academic terms, could be deemed a complete failure. His personal qualities were outstanding – he was kind, reliable (as exemplified by the fact that he rose at 6 a.m. every day to tend the family's goats and pigs), musical (he played in the school band), had perseverance (he obtained and retained a part-time job for two years) and displayed enthusiasm and conscientiousness (he worked voluntarily in a local engineering firm, keeping regular working hours, in all his holidays).

If this lad left school with only the traditional report, he would have been severely handicapped. With a profile he would have a positive statement of real, significant achievement. There is a danger that in over-reaction to the threat posed by subjectivity, many youngsters could be penalised.

It is, however, essential that every effort should be made to alleviate the danger. Any profile design should recognise, and attempt to counter, the inherent flaws by removing generalised statements such as 'is capable of establishing mature friendships' (how can an outsider possibly know?) and 'shows leadership potential' (in whose estimation, what does it mean?).

These can be substituted with phrases which illustrate actual achievements: 'led with energy a group of fellow students on a field expedition', 'organised efficiently and co-ordinated a sponsored appeal for Oxfam'.

The difficulty in adopting this specific, rather than generalised, statement is that it can lead to lengthy lists. It must be a matter of compromise in order to eliminate the worst of the subjectivity, without giving birth to a mammoth.

To summarise, the element of subjectivity, inextricably interwoven in human personality, presents some dangers in the profiling of pupils. Should profiles therefore be emasculated, and all comments on personal qualities and other elements in the affective domain receive a veto? It would be easier to adopt that approach, but it is arguable that it would not serve the best interests of students (in any case, subjectivity does not relate only to the affective domain). The benefits are so worthwhile for so many students, that it is worth making a very serious attempt to iron out some of the obvious pitfalls, and to be aware of, and try to compensate for, some of the more intransigent problems.

5.4   Untrained or uncommitted staff

One of the pitfalls about which it is possible to speculate – but about which there is, as yet, little evidence – is the effect upon the profiling process of untrained, or possibly worse, uncommitted teachers.

Much of the early enthusiasm for profiles arises from the experience of committed, industrious teachers. Whilst there are many such individuals, there is no denying that there are many who are less than industrious, and who are rigid and hidebound in their approach to new ideas – who cling fiercely to their 'right' to perpetuate the traditional content and pedagogy to which they are accustomed.

The question is: if profiles *are* a significant step forward in giving youngsters a fairer deal in assessment and recording, will they survive exposure to implementation by such teachers? Is the instrument sufficiently strong to withstand the pressures exerted on profiling by the unbelieving? It could be that antagonistic, or even merely indifferent, teachers may produce something *worse* than we have at present.

This is a common problem with any new departure – that the early results are distorted by the enthusiasm and dedication of the protagonists. Is it fair to young people to subject them to the disadvantages which are inherent in a system whereby a greater part of their lives are exposed to public scrutiny, and where the arbiter of much which is included is uncommitted or uninterested?

One of the effects that such teachers could produce would be the devaluing of the formative process, which, as I have stated earlier, is the essence of the advantage of profiling – if this is reduced to a meaningless formality, it is quite conceivably less helpful to the student than existing reports.

The product, too, will inevitably suffer by comparison with those compiled with the assistance of committed staff. There could be discernible differences between the size and quality of profiles which may not reflect the degree of pupil interest (the usual interpretation for slender profiles). The production of meagre or inadequate profiles, resulting from insufficient thought and care during compilation, could disadvantage students seriously.

Teachers with the attitude 'I've no time for this rubbish – I have to teach my subject' may, if forced, produce the bare minimum, but will have given no more thought to the process than they do under the present system, and because of the greater exposure inherent in the system, may cause more damage to the student and undermine profiling itself. The comments of an indifferent teacher are readily recognisable under the old system, and can frequently be offset – it may not be so easy under a wholesale profiling system.

Even if teachers are not openly antipathetic, they may lack the necessary inter-personal skills required to take full advantage of the new approach. Young people present different images of themselves according to the degree of empathy which is established. It is not difficult to foresee the difficulties which would arise in discussion, negotiation and confidential exchange of information when confronted by a teacher who may be uncommitted, or may be willing but lacking in the necessary skills.

Problems arise on many fronts in this situation, but two major areas fraught with difficulty are

i. failure to listen (possibly adopting a directive, didactic approach)
ii. lack of skill in drawing out of youngsters the whole story.

The problems relating to lack of training are, in fact, less insurmountable than intransigent attitudes. It is possible, and indeed essential, to mount in-service education to help teachers to develop skills in this area. It has been a universal demand from all the teachers with whom I have discussed profiling that there should be more in-service education (see Chapter 4).

An illustration of the effectiveness of training in the preparation for profiling is discussed in Chapter 4.5. The adoption of an active tutorial work programme prior to profiling, whilst not claiming a 100% success conversion rate, led to a significant change in teacher attitudes.

If the problem is untrained, uncommitted teachers, then attempts must be made to provide sufficient training to overcome the first problem, in the hope that it will result in persuading the uncommitted.

5.5 Time

'How do we find the time to cope with profiles and do our jobs as well?' This is the most common reaction from teachers in institutions contemplating the introduction of profiles. It may not be the *first* reaction – this depends on the level of interest and degree of commitment to change in each individual case, but it is of universal concern.

The question of teacher time, together with that of resources, is of paramount importance to the teachers' associations. Most unions are in favour of the introduction of profiles into schools. The NUT, whilst supporting the concept of profiling: 'Thus the fundamental principle underlying the Union's commitment to profiles, as expressed in its policy statement of 1980, is that *all* the work of *all* the pupils in a school is worthy of being assessed and recorded', nevertheless suggest that local authorities should 'be aware of the following requirements: . . . extra non-teaching time for all staff',[7] while AMMA recommends 'The time taken to operate a thorough, professional and valid system of profiling or recording needs to be reflected in schools' staffing establishments.'[8] In the case of all union pronouncements supporting profiling there is one large proviso – that there should be adequate resourcing, and that it should be recognised that profiling will involve teachers in extra work, a factor which should be acknowledged by the provision of extra staffing in order to release some teachers' time.

Teachers who have yet to embark upon the profiling of pupils are often particularly concerned about the sheer practicalities involved in both negotiating with students and with producing the requisite paperwork. One teacher with experience in the classroom, who has now progressed to training others, remarked on the degree of antagonism founded in fear of the unknown, which often manifested itself in an almost physical aggression with raised voices and pointing fingers.

There is no doubt that there is a real problem surrounding the issue of teacher time, and that, in the early stages of innovation at least, extra time is involved. The difficulty arises when the issue is clouded by fears – and it is fear which is at the root of much of the uncertainty and negative response. The danger is that in an attempt to allay these fears, the very real problems run the risk of being 'massaged away', when the need is that they be confronted.

Nevertheless, it is still possible to achieve a good deal by attempting to solve some of the practical difficulties. When teachers say 'I can't possibly do more', the response could be 'No, but could you do different?'.

This challenges the very heart of what teachers have committed themselves to in their teaching; many have already begun to question what they are attempting to achieve in the classroom, and this questioning appears to strengthen rather than weaken the teacher's professional capability and confidence. It is, however, a threat to many individuals, and riding rough-shod over their sensibilities is not the best way of approaching the problem.

There is as yet very little independent evidence relating to precisely how much extra time, if any, is involved in profiling. One study by the City and Guilds of London Institute, specifically relating to their own profile, produced quite daunting figures, suggesting that approximately thirty minutes of teacher time should be devoted to each pupil per review (one or two reviews per term).[9] If this is multiplied by a class size of, say, thirty the results would indicate that teachers should be spending between fifteen and thirty hours per term on profiling for each class. In the eyes of most people this would be quite unacceptable, although it could be argued that a number of activities which are already, or should be, an integral part of teaching and learning would be incorporated into profiling.

More light will perhaps be shed on the issue of quantifying the time required by the research initiatives mounted by the South Western Profile Assessment Research Project, and the evaluation of pilot schemes proposed under the DES Pilot Projects (1985–8).

If there is to be any progress in the direction suggested earlier of 'what different' rather than 'what more', one of the first things which schools, colleges and teachers will have to do is to establish priorities. Many schools are already critically examining their curriculum. It is only a small step from this to an equally searching examination of aims and objectives of the whole teaching process. If assessment is to be relocated at the centre of all teaching and learning, then much of this assessment will inevitably take place within lesson time. The requirement will then be to formalise what many good teachers are already practising. Additionally, the establishment of priorities automatically implies the identification of areas which are not of the first order of importance. It is at these areas that a critical investigation must be directed in order to remove less essential areas of the curriculum, recording and reporting, or administrative tasks, in order to release time which may be used in profiling.

It is the concept of *replacing* some existing activities which reinforces the 'different use of the same time' rationale of those who plead that profiles need not impose excessive burdens. Opinion seems to be about equally divided between those who hold this view and those who regard it as a palliative obscuring the issue.

The issue of extra time, whether real or perceived, is of crucial importance, and is one which it would be unfair to leave to schools to solve alone. Both Local Authorities and the DES will have to face up to the implications and offer both guidance and practical help. If they, and society as a whole, decide that there should be a different order of priorities, with a form of assessment which involves the pupil, provides for formative interaction and offers every school leaver a worthwhile certificate, then it follows that something should be removed from the diet – perhaps a norm establishing the sitting of fewer examinations in order to release more time for other activities within the curriculum would provide a solution.

There is a danger that Pavlovian responses of 'no time' detract from the genuine problems associated with the time and resources required for successful profiling. There is widespread agreement amongst teachers already involved in profiling that the benefits which accrue make the work worthwhile.

5.6 Credibility

To what extent are profiles likely to achieve credibility in the eyes of the beholder – whether this be employer, YTS supervisor, parent, teacher or student?

This is a question which exercises many people contemplating the introduction of profiles. One teacher stated: 'You bring me a body of employers who say that they will accept these profiles and we'll do it. Otherwise the staff will merely think it a waste of time.'

The answer to that remark, at least in the early stages, is that this is not possible. They have not been tried in a sufficiently widespread exercise for any accurate prediction of employers' response to be made. The most that can be hoped for is that initial indications that employers are prepared to look favourably upon profiles will prove generalisable.

On the other hand, there is another way of answering the same question. Does it really matter what employers think, if the development of the formative process of interaction leading to enriched personal development is what is prized? This reverts to the earlier issue of the purpose of profiles, but some schools certainly adopt the attitude that the profile starts and ends with the youngster – if it helps them (and the implication is that the pupil accords the profile credibility), then the issue of credibility with employers is immaterial.

Credibility focusses attention on the whole question of who assesses – who records – who comments? If there is no validation of entries by teachers or other adults, will the profile be accorded or achieve credibility? An example of the failure of such a record to attain credibility can be found in the Swindon Record of Personal Achievement scheme, with its strong formative influence, but weak currency value.

A further issue which might be raised by those who question the credibility of profiles is the areas which are assessed, and how are they to be assessed? If a profile says 'shows leadership qualities', how has this judgement been arrived at? It is not only teachers who are concerned about this potential flaw, but users as well.

The logical progression from asking 'how was it assessed?' is 'what opportunities have been provided for the young person to display and, even more important, to develop this quality?'.

This is a crucial factor – if profiles are to gain credibility in the eyes of those both inside and outside school, then there must be explicit provision for the development of qualities which are to be assessed.

This has repercussions for the curriculum, and for the hidden curriculum. Youngsters will have to be given opportunities for using their own initiative, for participating in decision-making activities and for taking greater responsibility for their own lives. The arrangements for such qualities to be developed and the approach to their assessment will need to be part of the development if credibility is not to be undermined.

5.7 Ownership

Ownership was not a burning issue in the early days of profiles. Traditionally schools had always reported on pupils, and had kept records of those reports with equanimity. The early profiles were more extensive, more enlightened versions of these summative reports, but in only a few cases did the question of the pupils' right to own both the document and the information recorded play any part in the process.

Gradually, more and more people were forced to the conclusion that if the aim of a profile is to include the pupil in a *real*, and not merely cosmetic, involvement in assessment, recording and negotiation of learning targets, then the logical extension of this philosophy must be that decisions regarding the use and storage of information should rest with the student.

In the case of the Evesham profile, this ownership was extended to include not only physical ownership of the document, but responsibility for deciding whether to seek staff's validation of skills. There was no compulsion on any young person to complete the profile. In all fairness, however, it is easier to adopt an egalitarian approach when the profile is an adjunct to, rather than a replacement of, all other forms of recording and reporting.

As discussion and development of the philosophy underpinning profiling has developed, so more and more people have become convinced that the only rational decision is that ownership rests with the student. As recently as 1983 the Avon Profiles Working Party agonised over the question 'Who should own the profile?'. It was decided that the student should own it, but we really felt that this was a fairly radical step – as indeed it was.

Only eighteen months later the principle had become so well established that it is encapsulated in the DES Statement: 'The Secretaries of State believe that the final summary document should become the property of the pupil, who would be free to decide whether or not to show it to prospective employers and others.'[10]

This laudably open approach does, however, create a number of related problems:

a. How can total pupil ownership be reconciled with the schools' need to keep records? There are a number of wholly defensible reasons why schools need to keep records on individual pupils. Many schools are attempting to rationalise the proliferation of records kept within the school, and to incorporate them into the profiling activities of the school. This has the advantage of not only reducing the number of activities which are reproduced by several teachers, office staff, etc., but also of ensuring that such records as are kept are open (with some clearly specified exceptions), and accessible.

b. The dilemma which faces schools over pupil ownership is the extent to which they may copy, store and subsequently divulge information which may have been acquired in confidence during formative discussion. This raises considerable moral and ethical questions. On one hand, the prospect of information which they divulge during formative, interactive profiling being used in confidential reports may well inhibit trust between student and teacher – it reinforces earlier disquiet over the extent to which individuals' privacy should be invaded.

On the other hand, the school is placed in an extremely difficult position if it can *not* keep and use records, and the student could be at a disadvantage if a reference is subsequently needed.

c. This issue of the ethics of recording and reporting on individuals is not confined to the teaching profession and to profiles. It is an issue which rages in other disciplines with even more fervour than is yet evident amongst teachers. In the field of social work the British Association of Social Workers recommend that 'Limits should be set on the external disclosure of information. Social workers should not disclose information entrusted to them, to people or agencies outside their agency unless it is to the benefit of the person who entrusted the information, who has specified that disclosure should not be restricted.'[11]

The DES Statement attempts to overcome the problem of conflicting interests by suggesting that 'Schools should retain a master copy and meet reasonable requests for duplicate copies by pupils who need them. They should not however supply copies to anyone else without the pupil's permission.'

This does not, however, answer the dilemma facing schools of the extent to which they are entitled to record and use information relating to a pupil which has been obtained whilst profiling – it does not, for instance, address the issue of pupils' ownership of the copyright of material which they have written.

The question of ownership is far more complex than it first appears, and a great deal more thought needs to be directed towards the resolution of these complexities. Even within the teaching profession, there is often wide discrepancy between those who think that the profile must remain within the control of the individual, and those who feel, as one teacher remarked, 'Employers have a right to *demand* the truth.' This elicits the questions 'whose truth?' and 'what *is* truth?'.

d. A subsidiary problem which may be linked to the issue of what to record and to whom the record should be divulged, is the question of how much of the profile compiled over a number of years is it right and proper to keep on file. There may be experiences, attitudes and comments which the student recorded at the age of eleven which in no way reflect a realistic picture of the sixteen-year-old individual. The easy response is that if the student has ownership any part of the profile can be deleted or physically removed at any time, but this again may conflict with the school's need to keep records.

Perhaps a partial attempt to resolve the dilemma may be for the school to identify the principal areas in which it really *needs* to keep records (and it is arguable that a great many of those currently kept are quite unnecessary), to communicate these areas to the pupil and to make it clear that such records *are* being kept.

This is not more than a partial answer to a problem which has not yet revealed the full extent of the pitfalls which may become apparent as more and more institutions enter the field of profiling.

Summary

This chapter has investigated some of the more prevalent pitfalls associated with profiles. One of the great dangers is that in trying to fulfil all of the purposes discussed in Chapter 2, there is the risk of attempting to be 'all things to all men': the result is frequently a compromise which satisfies no one.

One of the less frequently identified pitfalls, but one which is the most potentially dangerous, is the use of profiles as agents of social control, social-ising young people into an acceptance of failure under the influence of a benevolent despotism. A consensus view that one is only capable of x or y is far more difficult to rebel against than the individual judgement of a teacher who can be written off as 'biased' or 'stupid'. It may seem as if there is no escape in the mind of the youngster.

Allied to this danger, but more frequently recognised by teachers, is that of subjectivity. Every effort must be made to minimise the damage which may be done to students by the subjectivity which inevitably colours the perceptions of teachers.

There is no doubt that in the eyes of many teachers, the issue of time is the over-riding concern. There is fear that they will be even more over-burdened than they are at present, and in a climate of unrest and dissatisfaction with salary awards, new, potentially threatening, innovations are not welcome to some. The extent to which profiles can substitute for other activities, making a different use of existing time, rather than extra time, is discussed. Problems arising from untrained or uncommitted staff are also considered – would pupils profiled by such teachers emerge with a worse experience and certificate than they have at present?

Finally two issues, rather than pitfalls, are considered: credibility ('will users grant profiles the degree of credibility they require in order to become universally accepted?') and ownership ('who owns the profile?'). Most protagonists now accept that the pupil should own the profile, and this view is endorsed by the DES.[12] However, there are sub-issues such as who physically keeps the profile, to what extent is confidential material available for use in references, to what extent does the pupil control the copyright of any material in the profile?

There is no easy solution to the problems highlighted in this section on pitfalls. The most that can be achieved is to be aware of the difficulties, to confront them and to attempt to ameliorate them, to compare with the possible benefits highlighted in the 'purposes' section (Chapter 2) and to try to take full advantage of these benefits whilst avoiding the worst traps in the pitfalls.

Notes

1. See Schools Council, *Records of achievement*, Terry Swales, Schools Council (occasional paper), 1981.
2. Department of Education and Science, and Welsh Office, *Records of achievement: a statement of policy*, 1984.
3. Ranson, S., Towards a tertiary tripartism: new codes of social control and the 17+, in Broadfoot, P.M. (ed.), *Selection, certification and control*, Falmer Press, 1974.
4. Stronach, I., *Pictures of performance*, School of Education, University of East Anglia, 1983 (unpublished working paper).
5. Broadfoot, P.M., From public examinations to profile assessment: the French experience, in Broadfoot, *Selection certification and control*.
6. Stronach, *Pictures of performance*.
7. National Union of Teachers, *Pupil profiles: a discussion document*, 1983.
8. Assistant Masters and Mistresses Association, *Profiles and records of achievement: an introduction to the debate*, 1983.
9. City and Guilds of London Institute, *An evaluation of a basic abilities profiling system across a range of education and training provision*, 1982.

10. Department of Education and Science, and Welsh Office, *Records of achievement.*
11. British Association of Social Workers, *Effective and ethical recording*, 1983.
12. Department of Education and Science, and Welsh Office, *Records of achievement.*

Chapter 6

What should profiles include?

This chapter considers first: what existing profiles include, and second: what *should* profiles include.

In the introduction, a profile was defined as: 'a document which can record assessments of students across a wide range of abilities, including skills, attitudes, personal achievements, personal qualities, and subject attainments; it frequently involves the student in its formation, and has a formative as well as a summative function.' There is, however, no universal agreement that inclusion of *all* these elements is essential in any profile, though it is assumed that most will be included.

6.1 Existing profiles

As part of research carried out in Spring 1983,[1] the format and content of a large number of profiles, some developed by national bodies, and others the result of independent initiatives within individual schools, were analysed.

The results, offering purely factual information, are presented in a series of tables denoting:

Fig. 6.1: Table A: Profiles considered
Fig. 6.2: Table B: Breakdown of profile content
Fig. 6.4: Table C: Skills breakdown
Fig. 6.5: Table D: Personal qualities

Table A: Profiles considered
Of more than one hundred profiles examined, twenty have been selected as being representative of the range available. The very wide variation is immediately apparent – some documents are called 'reports', some 'profiles', some 'achievement records'. They have been included because they fulfil the criteria outlined in the definition above.

Other variations include the vastly differing size – ranging from single A4 sheets to thirty-six-page, leather-bound dossiers (J). Some have been produced as a result of regional or national initiatives (A), some are the product of commercial development by examination boards (P, N, O), whilst others are the result of individual schools (H).

		A-L Schools M-R Post School Training or External Bodies		
Name	Document Title	Number of pages	When compiled	Student Contribution
A	School Leaving Report	4	On leaving	None
B	16+ Profile	8	On leaving	2 pages
C	Pupil Profile	9+	On leaving	1+ pages
D	Achievement Certificate	11	On leaving	1 page
E	16+ Pupil Profile (1983)	7+	On leaving	1+ pages
F	16+ Pupil Profile (1981)	7	On leaving	1 page
G	Pupil Profile	9	On leaving	1 page
H	Personal Achievement Record	8	Continuously	2 pages
I	Student Profile	3+	Continuously	1+ (half)
J	Diploma	up to 36	Continuously	11 pages
K	Leavers Profile Report	3	On leaving	None
L	Year Progress sheet (draft)	1	Half yearly	None
M	Profile	12	On leaving	1 page
N	365 Profile Report	8	Periodic	Extensive
O	YTS Final Profile	4	Joint agreement	Extensive
P	Practical Communication Profile	2	At completion	None
Q	Profile Report	5	At completion of year	None
R	Profile & Review Book	7+	Weekly	Extensive

Table A: Profiles Considered

Fig. 6.1

The most significant finding in Table A, apart from the identification of discrepancy in size, is the column indicating when the document is completed. The time at which the profile is completed reveals an insight, however crude, into the extent of formative processes in the profile. Where documents are completed on leaving, they are less likely to place great emphasis on teacher–student continuing interaction in profiling and assessment. This is not an entirely reliable guide to the formative nature of the profile; it is more likely to be an illustration of the point made in Chapter 4, that many of the early developers of profiles initially seeking better *summative* profiles, soon learned that the benefits extended far beyond merely producing fuller reports.

Therefore, whilst school profiles originally concentrated largely on 5th-year students, recognition of these benefits prompted many schools to extend profiling into the 4th year. It is now accepted by many participants (and by DES) that ideally, profiling should commence in the 1st year – a dramatic shift of emphasis in a very short time.

Table B: Profile content

Table B analyses the overall categories included in the sample profiles. The greatest area of agreement on content is found in sections relating to subject assessment and cognitive skills. Almost all profiles contained reference to cognitive and social skills. Five profiles did not list subjects studied, although in four cases this could be compensated for in the staff entries, and in one (C) examination certificates were included. One profile (D) included a syllabus synopsis for each subject (see Fig. 6.3).

Profiles intended principally for the post-sixteen sector were heavily weighted towards cognitive and social skills.

A-L Schools M-R Post School Training or External Bodies

Name	Subjects Studied	Cognitive	Personal & Social	Personal Achievements	Community Service	Examinations Awards: Results obtained and anticipated	Attendance Punctuality	Staff	Pupil
A	✓	✓	✓					✓	
B	✓	✓	✓	✓	✓	✓	✓	✓	✓
C		✓	✓	✓	✓	✓	✓	✓	✓
D	✓	✓	✓	✓	✓	✓	✓	✓	✓
E	✓	✓	✓	✓	✓		✓	✓	✓
F	✓	✓	✓		✓			✓	✓
G	✓	✓	✓	✓		✓			
H	✓	✓	✓	✓	✓	✓	✓		
I	✓		✓	✓		✓	✓	✓	✓
J	✓	✓	✓	✓	✓	✓	✓	✓	✓
K	✓	✓	✓				✓	✓	
L	✓	✓	✓				✓		
M		✓	✓		✓	✓		✓	✓
N	✓	✓	✓	✓		✓			
O		✓	✓	✓		✓			
P		✓	✓					✓	✓
Q		✓	✓					✓	✓
R	✓	✓	✓	✓		✓	✓	✓	✓

Table B: Breakdown of Profile Content

Fig. 6.2

Approximately half of the sample profiles commented factually on attendance and punctuality, and a similar number included sections for the recording of personal achievement.

Only one example, provided by Comberton Village College, adopted the negotiated approach involving student participation ranging beyond solely student recording of experience. (Student–teacher negotiation is discussed more fully in Chapter 3.) However, a significant development in the relatively short time since this survey was carried out is the number of profiles originally consisting of teacher comment only which now include student contribution.

The profile contents table is broken down further to expose skill categories and personal qualities in greater detail.

Table C: Skills breakdown
When the profiles were analysed in terms of skills there was remarkable unanimity regarding the inclusion of communication skills (listening, speaking, reading, writing) and numeracy. Skills which were assessed in some, but not all, profiles included 'co-ordination', 'manual dexterity', 'creativity' and 'visual understanding' (sometimes called graphicacy – the ability to interpret graphs and diagrams) (see Fig. 6.4). It appeared that schools were less likely to comment upon visual understanding than colleges and outside bodies. Interestingly the latest RSA General profile includes the category 'ability to establish priorities'.

SUBJECT TUTOR REPORT

MOTOR VEHICLE ENGINEERING

    The two year course in
Motor Vehicle Engineering leads
to a C.S.E. Mode 1 examination
in two parts, one theoretical
and one practical.

    Candidates need to have a
working knowledge of a car
engine and transmission, the
electrical components, the
brakes and the construction
of the vehicle. They must
be aware not only how a
component works, but also
the symptoms of component
failure and its rectification.

    All candidates must
become involved in the
practical maintenance of a
vehicle, and be able to perform
routine service tasks. The
use of the correct tools and
safety precautions are all
taken into account when marking
these tasks.

    Candidates must also be
aware of the laws governing
the use of a vehicle on the
road and current M.O.T.
regulations.

NAME OF
PUPIL:-   ....

FORM:-   ....

LEVEL OF ACHIEVEMENT:-

C.S.E. Mode 1

ANTICIPATED FINAL EXAMINATION GRADE:-

         ....

SUBJECT TUTOR'S COMMENTS:-

SIGNED:- ....

DATE:-   ....

Fig. 6.3: A syllabus synopsis from Norton Priory School

A-L Schools / M-R Post School Training or External Bodies	Listening	Speaking	Reading	Writing	Number	Other e.g. French	Co-ordination	Manual Dexterity	Visual Understanding and Expression	Creativity	Method of Presenting Assessment (If grid, number of options)
A	✔	✔	✔	✔	✔		✔	✔	✔	✔	Grid (4)
B	✔	✔	✔	✔	✔		✔		✔	✔	Comment Bank
C	✔	✔	✔	✔	✔	✔	✔	✔	✔	✔	Comment Bank
D	✔	✔	✔	✔	✔	✔			✔	✔	Tutor Comments
E	✔	✔	✔	✔	✔	✔	✔	✔	✔	✔	Grid (3) & Comments
F	✔	✔	✔	✔	✔	✔			✔	✔	Grades A-E
G	✔	✔	✔	✔	✔		✔	✔			Criterion Checklist
H	✔	✔	✔	✔	✔	✔	✔	✔	✔		Criterion Checklist
I	✔	✔	✔	✔	✔	✔	✔	✔	✔	✔	
J		✔	✔	✔	✔	✔	✔	✔	✔	✔	Grades A-E
K	✔	✔	✔	✔	✔			✔		✔	Grid (3)
L	✔	✔	✔	✔	✔			✔		✔	Grades A-E
M	✔	✔	✔	✔	✔		✔	✔	✔	✔	Grid (4) & Comments
N	✔	✔	✔	✔	✔		✔	✔	✔	✔	Grid (4) + example of work
O	✔	✔	✔	✔	✔		✔	✔	✔	✔	+ experience checklist
P	✔	✔	✔	✔					✔	✔	Criterion Checklist
Q	✔	✔	✔	✔	✔		✔	✔	✔	✔	Grid (4) & personal recording
R	✔	✔	✔	✔	✔		✔	✔	✔		Varied

Fig. 6.4: Skills breakdown

Table D: Personal qualities
This is the most delicate and sensitive area in profiling. It is not, therefore, surprising that there was considerable variation in the categories included. Nevertheless, in spite of the difficulties, most profiles elected to include at least some personal qualities.

The most common were 'social relationships', 'perseverance', and 'initiative'. Least popular were 'courtesy', 'maturity' and, surprisingly, 'adaptability/flexibility' (see Fig. 6.5).

It is noticeable that with the heightened awareness of issues surrounding personal qualities assessment, there is very little evidence of comment on 'honesty'. There appears to be a general reluctance to comment upon so nebulous and potentially damaging an area.

These tables are presented not as a definitive analysis of profile format and content per se, but rather they have sought to convey the wide-ranging, diverse nature of profiles and profiling, and to simplify a confusing scene. Most profiles are an amalgam of differing types and approaches. The tables should help to provide a framework which can be used to examine individual profiles, and which can also be used to consider what *should* be included in profiles.

6.2   What *should* profiles include?

The intention in this section is not to be prescriptive, but nevertheless certain recommendations are offered, which may be adopted or disregarded. The existence of concrete suggestions may prove helpful in clarifying ideas, even if they do not match the specific requirements of your organisation.

Four major areas are crucial in both formative and summative profiling:
a. personal qualities
b. personal achievements
c. cross-curricular skills
d. academic attainment.

Throughout each of these sections the contribution of the student is vital. Profiles can offer a better, fuller picture of the individual even without student contribution, but the active participation of the student transforms the picture from black and white into colour.

a. Personal qualities
This for many teachers is the real sticking point. It is the area which most threatens to impinge on the individual's privacy; it is the area which is most susceptible to bias and subjectivity; it raises questions about confidentiality. Many teachers are extremely uneasy about the ethical question of commenting publicly on student personality, while others are concerned about the wisdom of being held publicly accountable for their judgements in so sensitive an area.

Nevertheless, as was pointed out in Chapter 4, in spite of the difficulties and

A-L Schools / M-R Post School Training or External Bodies	Adaptability Flexibility	Perseverance Reliability	Initiative	Self-confidence	Self Awareness	Leadership	Co-operation	Social Relationships	Courtesy	Decision making	Appearance	Honesty, Truthfulness	Responsibility	Maturity	Method of Presenting Assessment
A		✔	✔												Grade A-E
B	✔	✔	✔	✔	✔										Comment Bank
C	✔	✔	✔			✔	✔				✔	✔	✔	✔	Comment Bank
D		✔	✔	✔	✔	✔	✔	✔	✔	✔	✔		✔	✔	Tutor Comments
E	✔	✔	✔	✔		✔		✔							Comment Bank
F		✔	✔			✔		✔	✔			✔			Grade A-E
G				✔			✔	✔			✔	✔	✔		Criterion Checklist
H				✔	✔						✔		✔		Criterion Checklist
		✔		✔		✔	✔	✔			✔		✔		Pupil/teacher statements
J		✔	✔	✔						✔					Grade A-E
K		✔	✔					✔							Grid (4)
L							✔	✔							Grade A-E
M		✔		✔				✔	✔						Grid (4)
N	✔	✔	✔	✔	✔	✔	✔	✔	✔	✔			✔	✔	Grid (4) + example of work
O	✔	✔	✔	✔	✔	✔	✔	✔	✔	✔			✔	✔	+ experience checklist
P															Criterion Checklist
Q							✔						✔		Grade A-E Grid & personal recording
R	✔	✔	✔	✔	✔	✔	✔	✔	✔	✔	✔	✔	✔	✔	Varied

Table D: Personal Qualities

Fig. 6.5

potential dangers, it is in the interests of most young people that personal qualities should be included in a profile. Too many students with sterling qualities, but little in terms of academic potential, are penalised because they do not receive credit for their most useful attributes.

The inclusion of personal qualities is advocated, but it is also recommended that the qualities to be included, and the method of assessing them, should be rigorously scrutinised in order to mitigate any damaging effects. Some youngsters may be penalised by unfair reporting, but the alternative is the prospect of a greater number of students being penalised as a result of the omission of their best attributes.

The argument against those teachers who feel it is wrong to comment lies in the fact that we already *do* comment on these things, but perhaps in too brief records or reports, or in a throwaway manner, perhaps in the staff room, where the remark may inadvertently colour the perceptions of other members of staff without there being any opportunity for the youngster to know or influence the outcome. So, since it is already taking place, let it be done as *professionally* as possible and as *openly* as possible.

How, then, to achieve this professionalism, and remove the elements of bias and subjectivity? Possible solutions include:

i. Awareness-raising – the first step is already taken when the dangers are faced and openly discussed.

ii. Institute a programme of in-service training which will encourage teachers to look at the difficulties and to find ways of overcoming them. (A useful means of setting the right climate has been found by some schools in the use of group tutorial work.)

iii. Ensure that a number of teachers, and not only one, are involved in the assessment of personal qualities. This helps to obviate the danger of personality clashes: if the outcomes differ, this is a legitimate result.

iv. Involve the pupils in their own assessment of personal qualities. This is a concept which is gaining credence, but which is still in its infancy. It seems obvious to involve the one person who should be in the best position to offer an illuminating perspective. If one of the aims of profiling is to encourage individuals to know themselves better, it would seem unwise to exclude them from one of the processes best able to help them achieve this.

v. One way of avoiding the inclusion of characteristics which would be considered damaging by the young person is to adopt the Avon procedure (see Chapter 3.2) of allowing the individual to select, from a prompt list, those categories which he or she particularly wishes to include, and encourage the youngster to comment first, followed by the teacher. This also allows for differences of opinion, which should be discussed, but should not be 'massaged away'.

vi. Try to avoid, as far as possible, entries which are based upon unsupported opinion. A better way is that suggested by the DES when it says: 'the greater extent to which personal qualities and skills can be inferred from concrete examples the more valuable it is likely to be to users',[2] for example, 'has demonstrated both reliability and conscientiousness by regularly visiting and shopping for an old lady for one year'.

vii. Avoid making generalised statements which may infer a global judgement. Try to make comments as specific as possible.

viii. Describe experiences without making judgements on them.

b. Personal achievements

Personal achievements form an important part of the student profile. The recognition of, and giving credit for, achievements is significant in boosting self-confidence and enhancing the student's self-image. The DES actually entitle their Statement of Policy *Records of achievement*. It would, therefore, regardless of educational reasoning, seem illogical to omit an element which the DES deem sufficiently important to adopt as a title.

Individuals' personal achievements can be recorded in a number of ways – for instance the teacher may wish to record achievements which have been observed. However, in my view personal achievements are known best by the individual and should be recorded by that person.

Once it is accepted that recording achievements is a desirable feature of the profile, and that they should in the main be recorded by the student, there are still a number of alternative approaches to recording. Some schools provide a single sheet for student comments to be included at the end of the profile. There are differences even within this type, in that some institutions allow free access and completion over a period, whilst others organise a 'recording day' – everyone sits down together and completes the form at the same time.

At the other end of the continuum is the level of student recording found in RPA and PPR (see Chapter 3). This relates to student interests, experiences and activities as well as to achievements, but the philosophy underpinning personal recording is reflected in a more detailed achievement record.

Not every school or college will want to engage in the extensive work involved in PPR, but there is a great deal to be gained from following some of the principles involved (see Chapter 3).

The recording of personal achievements is unquestionably a vital part of the formative profiling process, but mere recording, without some associated tutorial involvement and guidance, will not produce the most beneficial results. If supportive guidance is part of the scheme, then personal recording is not only one component of the profile, but can help the student to a greater self-knowledge and self-esteem, which will hopefully influence other elements of the profiling process.

One example of the way in which counselling can be made effective is given in the PPR handbook (see Fig. 6.6).

The view that recording personal achievement is essential to good profiling is a little more complex, however, when taken in conjunction with the formative–summative debate. There seems little argument against the inclusion of personal achievement in the formative profile: the debate centres more on the question of whether it should be included in the final summative version, and if so, 'how much?' and 'in what form?'.

This must be answered according to individual circumstances, but the following suggestions are offered:

i. The recording of personal achievement is an essential and integral part of the process and should be pupil controlled, aided by careful, concerned guidance and endorsement by appropriate adults.
ii. Some contribution from the personal achievement section is necessary if the summative profile is to reflect accurately the flavour and principles informing the whole profile.
iii. In keeping with the philosophy that profiling is student centred and seeks to develop greater autonomy and self-reliance, I suggest that the student should select and abstract those entries in the formative profile which

```
                    TUTORS  ROLE  IN  PRACTICE

                    P.P.R. Work Experience


    Date                     Details                    Signed


    8.2.84            Yesterday I went to my work         J.F. Stephens
                      experience as usual nothing much
                      happened.


By the end of a session with an experienced  P.P.R. tutor the following facts
had come to light:-

          i)   She arrived at work in an O.A.P. home at 7.30 a.m.

          ii)  She helped lay up breakfast for 70 O.A.P.'s and then served it.

          iii) She helped some of the people who could not feed themselves
               adequately.

          iv)  She then helped those that needed help to get to the lounge
               area and helped clear away the breakfast.

          v)   She was then given a pass key to the private bedrooms and
               cleaned, tidied and changed beds as required.


It became apparent she thought little of this and was unaware  of the personal
qualities that she demonstrated.  She was surprised that the tutor placed any
value on them.
```

Fig. 6.6: An extract from the PPR handbook for a fifth year girl living in Avon

    should be included in the summative.

iv. It is a matter for the institution to decide whether the entry should be handwritten by the individual, or typed or word-processed. In the interests of equity, and of ensuring a high standard of presentation, a professionally finished version is desirable.

c. Cross-curricular skills

The word 'skill' is currently fashionable, but it is often used loosely, without regard to a clear understanding of the terminology.

    The RPPITB report suggested that a skill is 'the ability to organise and carry out actions which are predetermined by the person possessing the skill with the conscious purpose of achieving ends he/she can predict or anticipate'.[3]

So there is a strong correlation between the intention to carry out a particular action and the expectation that the action will be accomplished not just on one isolated occasion, but that it is capable of being repeated as required.

Reference to 'basic' skills frequently includes communication skills, such as listening, speaking, reading, writing; numeracy; practical and graphic skills. All of these skills are cross-curricular, cutting across individual subject boundaries.

Competence in basic skills is needed in order to provide young people with the means to work towards a particular learning objective. They are not ends in themselves, but means of acquiring 'coping skills'. These are 'the range of skills that allow people to translate knowledge into effective action, and to co-operate with others',[4] and involve activities such as taking initiative, concentrating, giving instructions, taking decisions. More sophisticated skills are called for in activities such as observing, abstracting, analysing, recording and interpreting.

All of these different levels of skill combine to make 'competencies'. A competency is made up of a combination of skills, attitudes, knowledge and experience which helps to prepare young people for adult life.

Skills have to be learnt and practised and not just taught: a strong argument can be made in favour of establishing appropriate learning situations for students, to provide for the identification of skills, for their aquisition and for their practice.

Once again, selection must be left to the profilers concerned, but the following points are important:

i. Assessment of cross-curricular skills is central to the philosophy of profiling – it assesses skills across the barriers of subject boundaries, and, by assessing them, makes it explicit to teachers and students that they are important.

ii. Developing cross-curricular assessment skills requires support and training. It is unreasonable to expect teachers to adopt a completely new approach to teaching and assessment without such in-service support.

iii. Inclusion of cross-curricular skills in the teaching and assessment programme helps to encourage teachers to look at the whole person rather than the performer in a specific subject.

iv. Aquisition of cross-curricular skills may have a far greater degree of relevance for many young people than the traditional subject-based assessment which has so often labelled them as failures.

v. An appropriate environment and opportunity for developing skills needs to be provided.

In this way profiles broaden the base of educational assessment so that the picture which can be presented relates to the whole individual.

d. Academic attainment
It is important that assessment of academic attainment be included in both

formative and summative profiling. Without academic attainment the profile becomes emasculated – it runs the risk of undermining its credibility and of being seen as 'one of those easy option exercises for the less able'.

The importance of profiling as a tool in diagnostic assessment has been discussed in Chapter 4. Without the inclusion of academic attainment in the profile, there would be neither the motivation nor the opportunity to engage in the type of diagnostic assessment accompanied by discussion and the identification of appropriate remedial strategies advocated.

The inclusion of academic attainment in formative profiling offers a major opportunity to involve students in setting their own learning objectives, in diagnosing their strengths and weaknesses and in negotiating their curriculum – not capitulation (there will always be certain constraints which will need to be recognised by student and teacher), but negotiation.

The difficulty arises in transferring information gathered during the formative process onto a summative product. If the final profile is necessarily limited in space, there must be some way of compressing the wealth of material available.

Is it to be conflated into grades for 'effort' and 'attainment'? To do this could run counter to the spirit in which the process has developed.

Since assessment of academic attainment is advocated, it is logical to extend the argument to include examination results. This is not entirely straightforward, however; it is complicated by the question of whether *predicted* examination grades should be included.

On the one hand, profiles emphasise positive achivement, personal development and progress, and are not intended to be predictive; on the other hand, assessing future examination attainment implies an overtly predictive, sorting process which is instrumental in allocating life-chances. The philosophy of the two approaches is in conflict, and a strong argument can be made for excluding the prediction of future results, even where students are leaving school or college before receiving the results of their examinations. Recording of actual examination grades already accomplished is a different matter. In terms of simple logistics, for the majority of students the results of GCE and CSE examinations will not be available when profiles are presented. In the case of those who have either taken examinations early, who are receiving a profile in the 6th form, or who are students in a College of Further Education and may already have received either academic or vocational awards, the case may well be different.

As with every other element of the profile, the ultimate decision must rest with the organisation concerned, but the following suggestions are made. In the formative profile:

i. Academic assessment should form an integral part of the profile.
ii. In addition to traditional assessment, diagnostic assessment should form an important part of the process.
iii. The resulting diagnosis should form the basis for discussion between teacher and taught.

iv. Academic objectives should at least be explained to the young person, and at best negotiated.

v. The individual, as well as the teacher, should be involved in assessing progress within subjects.

In the summative profile:

i. Predictions of external examination performance should not be included in a profile.

ii. Actual examination results, the results of graded tests, music examination, First Aid certificates, etc., may be included, although it may be preferable to include them in a separate folder.

iii. An abstract of the academic assessment carried out in the formative process should be presented. It may be that an agreed prose statement would be the fairest method of transferring such information.

Attendance and punctuality, although having less crucial implications, are still considered sufficiently important to include in most profiles. They may seem to be uncontroversial items but questions are raised by the method of their recording. For example:

Attendance – 'good', 'average' or 'poor' is not an adequate response – 'good' in whose eyes – on what criteria?

A more objective response can be given by using numerical evidence, rather than vague descriptors, for example:

Attendance: $\dfrac{96}{102}$

An exception should, however, be made for instances of notified illness in order that the luckless individual, normally punctilious about attendance, is not penalised for the unavoidable bout of 'flu!

6.3 What should be deliberately excluded?

This is a complex and delicate area, which needs to be thoroughly considered and discussed before the development of any profile. Some of the questions which might be addressed include:

i. Is the identification of negative characteristics and areas which can be improved crucial to the formative profiling process?

ii. Should negative comments be included in the summative profile?

iii. To what extent should such comments be tailored to soften any possible damage to the individual's self-esteem?

iv. Should categories such as 'honesty', which might lend themselves to defamatory statements, be included?

There are many other questions which could figure in such a list.

Perhaps the most important outcome is to recognise that there *are* categories which should not merely be omitted, but which should be excluded as the result of a deliberate policy decision.

Summary

This chapter has not only identified current practice, but has offered positive suggestions. It may be that these suggestions run counter to the approach favoured by individual institutions. However, if it either (a) offers positive guidance or (b) provides something concrete against which to direct argument, then it has fulfilled its purpose.

I have argued for the inclusion of personal qualities, personal achievements, cross-curricular skills and academic attainment. In each of these areas key issues for consideration before taking decisions are identified.

The inclusion of attendance and punctuality are advocated, with certain reservations, and attention is drawn to the fact that there are certain categories which should be deliberately excluded.

Notes

1. Hitchcock, G., *Profiles*, County of Avon Education Authority, 1984.
2. Department of Education and Science, and Welsh Office, *Records of achievement: a statement of policy*, 1984.
3. Rubber and Plastics Processing Industry Training Board, *The way forward: a practical proposal for introducing change in school curricula*, 1982.
4. *Ibid.*

Chapter 7

Practical guide to establishing a profiling system

This chapter brings together issues which have been raised in earlier chapters – the aim here is to extract the 'bare bones' from the meat of the book.

I do not wish to be presciptive about the ideal type of profile which should be implemented in any organisation. The essence of profiling is that it should be central to the learning process and should suit the school or college ethos. This does not preclude adopting or adapting part or all of a ready-made system. It *does* mean that the values of the organisation need to be established and that the profile accords with those values.

At the beginning of each section in this chapter, several major alternatives are identified. The arguments surrounding each of the alternatives are presented in tabular form. They represent a variety of views – the intention is to offer the basis for discussion, not to promote one philosophy. Issues covered include:

7.1 Of whom?
7.2 By whom?
7.3 For whom?
7.4 For what?
7.5 Of what?
7.6 When?
7.7 Where?
7.8 How?
7.9 Which type of assessment?
7.10 What format?

Adjacent statements are not in direct opposition to each other, they are merely lists of opposing views. At the end of your discussion of each area it may be decided that a combination of several approaches should be adopted.

At the end of each section is a small 'decisions' box; the decisions recorded here can be transferred to the larger matrix at the end of the chapter, in order to give a clear picture of the priorities established and decisions taken. This should provide a graphic representation of implications for your organisation.

7.1   Of whom?

Main alternatives:
a. All students?
b. Bottom 40% of the achievement range?
c. Students on vocational preparation courses only?

a. All students

Arguments for

  i. All students benefit from a more rounded curriculum and recognition of qualities beyond their academic attainment.
 ii. Everyone is entitled to a statement of achievement relating to their time in school.
iii. A statement is made about the policy and the ethos of the school: profiling is given a positive status.
 iv. Staff are encouraged to value the development of social skills and personal qualities.
  v. Modification of teaching styles is encouraged.

Arguments against

  i. It means more work for staff.
 ii. It involves reorganising the curriculum.
iii. New administrative procedures will have to be developed.
 iv. Students with good examination passes don't need profiles.
  v. Employers are only interested in 'O' levels.
 vi. Neither teachers nor pupils can spare the time from their academic studies.
vii. It would mean a complete change in teaching style.

b. Bottom 40% of the achievement range

Arguments for

  i. It gives the youngsters something special of their own.
 ii. It compensates for the lack of examination certificates.
iii. The curriculum can be geared especially to the needs of the less able, with particular emphasis on experiential learning.

Arguments against

  i. It is divisive – it categorises young people into those who succeed, and those who are 'profiled'.
 ii. It smacks of condescension.
iii. It inevitably assumes a low status in the eyes of staff and pupils.
 iv. This undermines the ability of profiles to generate enthusiasm and energy from staff and pupils alike, which is necessary if they are to work properly.

c. Students on vocational preparation courses (see also 1.5e and 1.5f)

Arguments for	*Arguments against*
i. It is easier to integrate assessment and curriculum into one cohesive package.	i. It separates 'sheep' and 'goats', offering pre-vocational students a separate, and often less prestigious certification.
ii. The assessment can be designed to relate specifically to the learning needs and perceived relevance of the students.	ii. Profiling should be about the whole person, and all people – it should not be divisive.
iii. The profile certificate offers those who are not likely to achieve many 'O' levels or CSEs a recognised certificate with standing and relevance in the outside world.	iii. Staff may view profiling as being the purlieu of teachers actually involved in the courses, and thereby overlook the value of developing skills and attitudes across subject boundaries for all students.
iv. It facilitates team teaching and cross-curricular teaching and assessment.	

Alternatives	Decision
All students	
Bottom 40%	
Vocational preparation students	

7.2 By whom?

Main alternatives:
a. Subject teachers?
b. Tutors?
c. Senior management?

a. Subject teachers (see also 6.2d)

Arguments for	*Arguments against*
i. In order to have a complete profile, subject assessment is essential, therefore subject teachers must be involved.	i. Subject teachers have enough to do teaching their subject – there is no time for anything else.
ii. Involving subject teachers in profiling will increase their use of diagnostic assessment within their own subjects.	ii. Academic standards will fall if time is stolen for profiling.
iii. Profiles can lead to improved relationships which in turn lead to a better atmosphere in the classroom.	iii. Many subject teachers do not know individual students sufficiently well to be able to comment.
iv. Better atmosphere in the classroom can provide opportunities for better attainment within subjects.	iv. Pupils and parents are more interested in getting good examination results than wasting time profiling in academic lessons.
v. Subject teachers can benefit from being encouraged to look across subject boundaries.	v. This sort of thing belongs on the pastoral programme – it's nothing to do with subject teachers.
vi. Teachers are encouraged to get to know their students better.	
vii. Profiling helps to break down the pastoral/academic divide.	

b. Tutors (see also 2.4)

Arguments for	*Arguments against*
i. Tutors know the students best.	i. The extra workload for the tutor is unacceptable.
ii. Tutors are in the best position to collate information.	ii. Collation of information is, in itself, a mammoth task regardless of the extra demands in terms of student contact time.
iii. Profiling reinforces and supports many of the concepts of social education and tutorial work.	iii. Many tutors do not have time to get to know their students well enough to profile.
iv. Tutorial work, in turn, enhances profiling.	iv. By making it clear that profiles are the province of tutors, the pastoral/academic divide is widened.
v. For less experienced tutors, the guidelines provided for profiling offer useful suggestions for utilising tutorial periods.	

Arguments for

vi. Profiling and tutorial work share a common ethos – the aims of formative profiling sit happily alongside the role of the tutor.

vii. By requiring tutors to set aside time for individual contact, it is almost inevitable that they will come to know their students better.

Arguments against

v. The tutor has to negotiate not only with students, but with other staff – a completely new element of the role.

c. Senior management

Arguments for

i. The involvement of senior management bestows status upon the activity.

ii. Management are able to acquire more information about students than is normally the case, and are brought into closer contact with the students.

iii. Staff involved in profiling are afforded a measure of support and reassurance that what they do is worthwhile.

iv. The heads' or deputies' contribution gives a feeling of 'validation'.

Arguments against

i. Management can't possibly know students well enough to contribute.

ii. Students and teachers will feel that their confidential formative work is being 'monitored'.

Alternatives	Decision
Subject teachers	
Tutors	
Senior management	

7.3 For whom?

Main alternatives:
a. The student?
b. Employers?
c. Teachers?
d. Parents?

a. The student

Arguments for

i. Profiles should be pupil-centred and aimed at the self-development of the individual.
ii. They should offer the *student* a worthwhile statement of activities and achievements in school.
iii. Profiles are primarily aimed at motivating students, increasing self-confidence and enhancing self-image – it must have most relevance to the student.

Arguments against

i. Profiles have to be accepted by employers if they are to have any value in the eyes of pupils, parents and teachers.
ii. Profiles should be primarily to help teachers streamline recording and reporting.

b. Employers

Arguments for

i. Profiles are really improved reports offering better information to help employers in selection.
ii. They help firms reduce wastage by reducing unsuitable appointments.
iii. They provide a basis for interviewing – for both employers and students.

Arguments against

i. Employers' attitudes are irrelevant in a time of high unemployment.
ii. To implement profiling as a more sophisticated screening device increases the danger of their use as tools of social control.
iii. The formative effect of profiles is undermined if students are aware that the end product will be used to sift and screen.

c. Teachers

Arguments for

i. It makes teachers' jobs easier by helping them get to know their pupils better.

Arguments against

i. Using the profile mainly in the teachers' interest gives teachers more power over pupils.

Arguments for	*Arguments against*
ii. Profiling helps teachers evaluate their teaching programme. iii. Profiles improve recording procedures. iv. They improve and rationalise reporting in the school. v. They provide teachers with more information.	ii. Invasion of privacy is less defensible if the process is undertaken for the benefit of the teacher rather than the pupil. iii. Students will not feel any sense of ownership, and therefore motivation, if the profile is principally for the teachers' benefit.

d. Parents

Arguments for	*Arguments against*
i. The more parental involvement in the students' school life the better, profiles can include parents in contributing, and in discussions, both with offspring and teacher. ii. Parents are entitled to better, fuller reports than they frequently receive. iii. Profiles offer parents a more accurate idea of their children's progress. iv. Profiles can provide a stimulus for communication between parent and child – something which is all too often neglected.	i. Students may not wish parents to receive detailed information about their experiences and confidential inner thoughts, which may have been recorded in formative profiling. ii. There is the same danger of invasion of privacy as exists if the profile is principally for the benefit of the teacher.

Alternatives	Decision
The student	
Employers	
Teachers	
Parents	

7.4 For what? (see also 4.1)

Main alternatives:
a. Formative development?
b. Summative statement?
c. Both?

a. Formative development
Arguments for

  i. Formative profiling can affect learning and enhance attainment.

  ii. It increases communication between student and teacher.

  iii. It improves relationships between teacher and taught.

  iv. It enhances student self-esteem.

  v. It improves student motivation.

  vi. It aids diagnostic assessment.

  vii. It records and assists progress.

  viii. It is a source of pride for the individual, and a recognition of personal achievement.

Arguments against

  i. Formative profiling has no external currency. Staff would be involved in hours of work for something employers won't use.

  ii. There is no external validation.

  iii. It is too intrusive – an invasion of students' private 'space'.

  iv. Teachers are there to teach, not to act as social workers.

  v. Many teachers do not have the requisite skills.

  vi. Some teachers do not know students well enough to be able to make valid comments.

b. Summative statement
Arguments for

  i. It offers students a worthwhile statement relating to their time in school or college.

  ii. It offers employers a more detailed statement relating to time in school or college.

  iii. Young people are given a goal towards which they can all strive.

  iv. Every young person is given the opportunity for a 'moment of glory' in a ceremonial 'rite de passage'.

Arguments against

  i. It is the process that matters, the end statement is irrelevant.

  ii. The profile should begin and end with the student.

  iii. We already have reports, why bother with anything else?

  iv. A necessarily brief document cannot do justice to all the formative work which a student has undertaken.

  v. Employers are not interested in profiles, they rely on examination results and their own tests.

c. Both

Arguments for

i. Formative profiling lacks punch and currency without the inclusion of a summative component.

ii. Summative profiles alone lack depth; the opportunity to involve assessment in the learning process is lost.

iii. The advantages of formative profiling and summative profiling (see above) are combined.

Arguments against

i. It is impossible to reconcile the philosophy of formative and summative profiling in one activity.

ii. It is not possible to condense or abstract several years activity into one brief statement.

iii. Who is to undertake the task of translating the formative process into a summative document?

Alternatives	Decision
Formative development	
Summative statement	
Both	

7.5 Of what? (see also Chapter 6)

Main alternatives:
a. Personal qualities?
b. Personal achievements?
c. Cross-curricular skills?
d. Academic attainment?

a. Personal qualities (see also 6.2a)

Arguments for

i. We already assess personal qualities in a haphazard, unstructured way, let's do it but make it as professional as

Arguments against

i. Assessment of personal qualities involves an unacceptable invasion of privacy.

ii. Questions of confidentiality and

Arguments for

possible.
ii. Credit is given to youngsters who may receive little in other areas.
iii. It helps to identify and develop 'desirable' qualities – sets a goal for which to aim.
iv. Omission of the best attributes of many young people penalises them unfairly.
v. Comments based on evidence, and involvement of students in the compilation of personal quality assessment helps to combat bias.
vi. If we are seeking to provide a fuller, more rounded picture of the individual, then personal qualities are an essential component.

Arguments against

legal liability are raised by public statements on personal qualities.
iii. Students are exposed to the dangers of subjectivity and bias.
iv. Teachers have no right to be judgemental about the personal qualities of students.
v. The danger of a 'big brother' element of social control is magnified.
vi. Comments may be destructive, which can have a damaging effect upon the young person's development.

b. Personal achievements (see also 6.2b)

Arguments for

i. It involves the student in the profiling process – a valuable outcome in itself, underpinning the formative intentions of the profile.
ii. It helps the student identify as real achievements activities which might previously have been undervalued.
iii. It provides more information which can form the basis of dialogue between student and teacher.
iv. It provides more information for employers.
v. It provides a more detailed source of information for teachers writing references.

Arguments against

i. Profiles are simply reports – students don't contribute to reports.
ii. Students can write anything – what proof is there that the entries are true?
iii. It takes valuable time when they could be doing something more useful.
iv. It is divisive – some students will have very full records, others will have little – some will record privileged activities, others will not have the opportunity to experience such things.

c. Cross-curricular skills (see also 6.2c)

Arguments for	*Arguments against*
i. Basic skills such as communication and numeracy are essential for the young person's survival in later life.	i. We are here to teach our subject – if we waste time on cross-curricular skills we won't be able to maintain academic standards.
ii. They need to be assessed if they are to gain a valued position within the curriculum.	ii. Cross-curricular skills are things that everyone picks up as they go along, they're nothing like as important as 'O' level maths, for example.
iii. Assessment of basic skills leads on to the acquisition of more complex skills such as decision-making, taking initiative.	iii. We're simply not trained to teach this sort of thing – leave it to the remedial department who are probably used to doing it.
iv. Inclusion of cross-curricular skills cuts across subject boundaries, and makes it clear to students as well as teachers that a cross-curricular approach is important.	iv. It's examination results that count, not all this 'rubbish'.
v. The teacher is encouraged to look at the whole person, rather than at the individual as a performer in a particular subject.	v. Kids with 9 'O' levels don't need anyone talking about their cross-curricular skills.

d. Academic attainment (see also 6.2d)

Arguments for	*Arguments against*
i. Subject teaching is an essential part of most curricula – to omit its assessment from the profile would be a nonsense.	i. There is already adequate testing and reporting of academic attainment.
ii. Without academic attainment, the profile loses credibility.	ii. Teachers are too busy teaching to be able to carry out systemic assessment and discussion with individuals.
iii. There is a danger that it would become seen as merely a consolation prize for the less able.	iii. Profiles are a pastoral activity – they shouldn't impinge on the academic work of the institution.
iv. The value of profiles as a tool for diagnostic assessment is negated if academic assessment is excluded.	
v. It encourages teachers and students to set learning objectives – students take more	

Arguments for

responsibility for their own
learning.
vi. Teachers gain valuable
feedback on the effectiveness of
the teaching programme.

Arguments against

Alternatives	Decision
Personal qualities	
Personal achievements	
Cross-curricular skills	
Academic attainment	

7.6 When? (see also 6.1)

Main alternatives:
a. Throughout the student's secondary career?
b. During the 4th and 5th years?
c. During the 5th year?
d. Post-sixteen?

a. Throughout the student's secondary career

Arguments for

i. The DES Statement of Policy
recommends that profiling
should take place from the first
year of secondary schooling.
ii. If an appropriate climate is to
be established in which
students are confident in
recording, and in exchanging
views with teachers, it is

Arguments against

i. If students are being 'profiled'
from the age of eleven, they
will be bored by the process by
the time they approach school-
leaving age.
ii. The time involved for all staff
profiling all students would be
excessive, and call for cut-backs
in other areas.

Arguments for	Arguments against

essential that they become accustomed to the process from an early age.

iii. Students need training in the skills required for profiling, just as teachers do. It is unrealistic to expect them to adapt to new methods of assessing themselves and interacting with teachers at a time when most young people are experiencing difficulty in adjusting to a new maturity.

iv. If there is a genuine belief in formative profiling, then the only logical course is for the process to involve all students of all ages.

iii. If profiling is considered to be mainly a summative exercise, profiling of youngsters of eleven and twelve is irrelevant.

iv. Profiling from the 1st year calls for such a radical reconsideration and reorganisation of the curriculum that it would be a practical impossibility.

b. During the 4th and 5th years

Arguments for	Arguments against

i. It is only the older student who have the necessary maturity for negotiation with teachers.

ii. This age group has its sights set on life after school – profiling makes more sense for them.

iii. The 4th year have a long haul to 5th-year examinations – profiling offers them an added interest in their progress.

iv. The interest and activities of teenagers are more appropriate for profiling than that of younger students.

v. Students who experience profiling only in the 5th year have called for it to be extended to the 4th year.

i. It is far too late to embark upon a complex process of personal recording cross-curricular skills and negotiation with teachers. These skills need to be acquired over time.

ii. There is no need to involve 4th years in profiling, they're not interested in leaving certificates until the 5th year.

iii. A time of physical and emotional change, coupled with the start of study for 5th-year examinations is a bad time to impose new activities and values upon young people.

c. During the 5th year

Arguments for

i. It is only in the 5th year that profiles have any relevance for students or teachers.

ii. Only 5th-year students have the necessary maturity to cope with profiling.

iii. It is only practicable to inaugurate major changes in small sections of the school at once – it is obviously most relevant in the 5th year.

iv. The greatest degree of dissatisfaction and disaffection occurs in the 5th year – it is clearly the place where 'emergency action' is most needed.

Arguments against

i. Any new system commenced in the 5th year, with a life of virtually two terms, is bound to be a superficial, cosmetic exercise.

ii. Young people are too wrapped up in thinking about examinations and careers to have time or energy for taking a new concept on board.

iii. The 5th year is far too late to develop the skills necessary for genuine formative profiling.

iv. Any profile commenced in the 5th year would assume a 'strap on' status – something imposed on top of existing school procedures rather than emanating from curriculum development.

d. Post-sixteen

Arguments for

i. CPVE particularly is a post-sixteen qualification which specifies that profiling shall play a major part in the assessment – therefore it is certain that post-sixteen profiles are here to stay.

ii. Other post-sixteen vocational courses adopt profiling as a major part of assessment.

iii. Students are more interested in receiving a certificate which will help them to gain employment at this age – if profiling is viewed as mainly a summative exercise it will have more relevance for this group.

Arguments against

i. If students are *only* to be profiled post-sixteen, the same arguments as those advanced in the '5th year' category apply – too late, too little and having too little effect on the formative development of the individual.

ii. If only pre-vocational young people are profiled, it endows the profile with second class status.

Arguments for	Arguments against

iv. Sixth formers who have participated in profiling earlier in their school lives often demand further profiles in the sixth form – their earlier profiles become redundant.

Alternatives	Decision
Throughout the student's secondary career	
During the 4th and 5th years	
During the 5th year	
Post-sixteen	

7.7 Where?

Main alternatives:
a. In the classroom?
b. In the tutorial base?
c. In the staffroom?

a. In the classroom

Arguments for	Arguments against

Arguments for	Arguments against

i. Assessment should be a central part of the learning process – profiling in the classroom ensures this.

ii. Assessment in the classroom ensures not only that assessment is a continuing part

i. It is counter-productive to divert valuable teaching time into profiling.

ii. It is not possible to concentrate on individual students during the lesson – what are the rest of the class supposed to do?

Arguments for	Arguments against

of the learning process, but gives the profile status in the eyes of teachers to whom only academic teaching is important.

iii. Diagnostic assessment is facilitated.

iv. A rolling programme, paying special attention to two or three students per lesson facilitates more accurate assessment, and helps subject teachers get to know their students better.

v. Students may support each other.

iii. It all adds to the existing workload of the subject teacher.

b. In the tutorial base

Arguments for	Arguments against

i. The tutor has most to do with profiling – it is the most appropriate place for profiling to take place.

ii. Negotiation between student and tutor is facilitated by use of the tutorial base.

iii. The tutorial/social education programme is enhanced by the central position of profiling within the tutorial system.

iv. It is the tutor who has the job of collating the profile – it is obviously easier if this can take place in the area where tutor and students most frequently meet.

i. Hiving off profiling into a separate tutorial base emphasises the pastoral/academic divide.

ii. Profiling is at least as much about subject and skills attainment as about tutorial-oriented activities.

iii. If profiling is to work, *all* staff need to be aware or involved – placing it in the tutorial base removes the incentive for staff involvement.

c. In the staffroom

Arguments for	Arguments against

i. Assessment has always taken place in the staffroom in free periods and after school.

ii. It's the only chance teachers have of writing assessments on

i. Assessment should be student-centred and placed at the centre of the learning process – how can this happen in the staffroom?

Arguments for	*Arguments against*

Arguments for

students – they're too busy teaching the rest of the time.
iii. Teachers need peace and quiet to be able to concentrate on making proper assessments.

Arguments against

ii. By definition, staffroom assessments are summative – what about formative profiling?
iii. Staff are encouraged to adopt a narrow range of stereotyped assessments if they are merely 'filling in' profiles as if they were reports.
iv. Improved communication and relationships are precluded by this approach.

Alternatives	*Decision*
In the classroom	
In the tutorial base	
In the staffroom	

7.8 How?

Main alternatives:
a. Objective testing?
b. Teacher judgements?
c. Student–teacher negotiation?
d. Student recording?

a. Objective testing

Arguments for

i. Users would place greater weight upon evidence produced as a result of objective testing.
ii. Grade-related criteria and criterion-referenced assessment are gaining prominence – it would seem sensible to include their use within the profiling

Arguments against

i. The connotations associated with the existing examination system would inhibit many students – the profile would seem like yet more examinations.
ii. The motivational effect arising from the recognition of

Arguments for

process.

iii. The danger of subjectivity and bias is greatly reduced.

iv. Standardised tests are easier to organise than individualised, negotiated profiling.

Arguments against

personal achievements, and student–teacher dialogue would be nullified.

iii. The necessary objective tests required to assess all areas incorporated into the profile are simply not available.

b. Teacher judgements

Arguments for

i. The teacher is in the best position to be able to make judgements about the student's work, progress, and personal qualities.

ii. Teachers have great experience of assessing young people's attributes, and of making comparisons in terms of standards achieved.

iii. It is less time-consuming for teachers to make the judgements than to embark upon negotiation with students.

Arguments against

i. This merely extends and perpetuates the old reporting system.

ii. It leaves the student wide open to the risks of bias and subjectivity, and is worse than that encountered in reports due to the more detailed nature of the profile.

iii. The unchallengeable nature of teacher comments associated with the point made in (ii) means that the potential for profiles to act as agents of social control is exacerbated.

iv. Without student involvement in interactive dialogue, the effects of formative profiling in terms of increased motivation, enhanced self-esteem, etc., are negated.

c. Student–teacher negotiation (see also 3.2)

Arguments for

i. Student–teacher interaction increases communication between the two.

ii. This almost inevitably leads to improved relationships.

iii. Student feedback gives teachers valuable information about the

Arguments against

i. Students do not have sufficient maturity to negotiate their own assessments.

ii. They would not be honest in their self-assessment.

iii. It is far too time-consuming.

iv. Where personality clashes

Arguments for	*Arguments against*
effectiveness of their teaching programme.	occur, the system would be unworkable.
iv. It increases motivation, particularly amongst those most disaffected and disillusioned.	v. Staff need training in the skills necessary for negotiation.
	vi. Agreement in what is to be used as evidence may be difficult to achieve.

d. Student recording (see also 3.1)

Arguments for	*Arguments against*
i. The question of relevance to students' interests is automatically answered – what is recorded is the students' choice.	i. Student recorded profiles have no currency.
ii. The greatest motivating force is generated when work is student-initiated.	ii. The evidence presented has little in the way of validation – how reliable, truthful, honest would it be?
iii. Personal recording, accompanied by skilled guidance, is the most effective tool in enhancing student self-esteem and self-image.	iii. There are no academic requirements in terms of accuracy and presentation.
iv. Personal recording allows the less able to produce valuable, recognised work which can be attractively presented – they have something of which they can be proud.	iv. Only trained staff would have the skills necessary to draw the best from students.
	v. One of the guiding principles of wholly student recorded profiles is that the recorded material is confidential to the student. How does this marry with the requirements of a public profile?
	vi. More able students are far more interested in working towards public examinations than spending time recording.

Alternatives	*Decision*
Objective testing	
Teacher judgements	

Alternatives	Decision
Student–teacher negotiation	
Student recording	

7.9 Which type of assessment? (see also 4.2)

Main alternatives:
a. Norm-referenced?
b. Criterion-referenced?
c. Ipsative?

a. Norm-referenced
Arguments for

i. Norm-referencing is familiar to students, parents, teachers and employers.
ii. It helps in the selection process.
iii. It helps to make comparisons between members of a group.
iv. It ranks students in order of achievement.
v. It looks at a spread of attainment, not just at 'those who can' and 'those who can't'.
vi. An element of competition is healthy – it has a motivating effect on many young people.

Arguments against

i. Norm-referencing is divisive – it reinforces feelings of failure.
ii. There is not necessarily any relation to outside standards – a student may be top in a remedial group, but bottom in the 'A' stream.
iii. Norm-referencing ranks across a broad range of objectives – it gives no idea of the mastery of individual elements.
iv. The competitive atmosphere created is contrary to the prevailing ethos which encourages co-operation.
v. Because comparison is made within a particular group, standards may slip up or down.

b. Criterion-referenced
Arguments for

i. Criterion-referencing gives information about attainment in comparison with a predetermined standard.

Arguments against

i. It is difficult to offer a sufficiently wide spread of criteria to offer meaningful goals to the whole ability

Arguments for	Arguments against
ii. The clear identification of mastery levels allows students to aim for mastery of specific criteria.	range.
	ii. It is difficult to implement unless objectives can be clearly identified and performance measured.
iii. It is important for progression from one level to the next, ensuring that a student has grasped one important pre-requisite before progressing to the next stage.	iii. Criterion-referencing may restrict the curriculum to the teaching of objectives.
iv. It enables teachers to identify how many of the class have achieved and understood a specific objective.	iv. Criteria are not necessarily allied to any external standard.
v. Criterion-referencing fosters co-operation rather than competition.	v. Some people view criterion-referencing as an easy option – not 'proper' testing.
vi. It is much fairer – the emphasis is on 'can do' rather than 'can't do'.	vi. It can still end up comparing students – it is simply the basis of comparison that is different.
vii. It provides a useful basis for diagnosis and guidance.	

c. Ipsative (measuring the student against individual past performance)

Arguments for	Arguments against
i. Ipsative assessment accords closely with the philosophy and purposes of formative profiling – personal development, motivation and improving individual attainment.	i. How is the base line, from which comparisons of individual progress are made, to be established in the first place?
ii. The important feature of ipsative assessment is that it measures and encourages *progress* in all areas.	ii. There is no point of reference for parents or users.
iii. It removes the temptation to make invidious comparisons between individuals.	iii. Self-referenced assessment is not adequate when basic competence has to be measured – e.g. the dentist or electrician is required to demonstrate more than that he has made progress!
iv. It encourages students to co-operate, and help each other towards improving attainment.	
v. By removing artificial	iv. The student is not prepared for the harsh realities of the external examination system.

Arguments for

    categorisation, it assists
teachers to concentrate on
developing the full potential of
the individual.

Arguments against

v. It is unacceptable as a form of
summative assessment.

NB. These alternative forms of assessment are not clear-cut alternatives.
There is often a considerable degree of 'blurring the edges'.

Alternatives	*Decisions*
Norm-referenced	
Criterion-referenced	
Ipsative	

7.10   What format? (see Chapter 3 for more detail)

Main alternatives:
a. Student recording?
b. Checklists?
c. Comment banks?
d. Grids?

a. Student recording (see also 3.1)
Arguments for

i. Student recording is entirely
consistent with the aims of
formative profiling.

ii. It helps to enhance self-esteem
and encourages recognition of
positive achievements.

iii. The process helps to improve
communication between teacher
and taught. Personal recording
can result in the student
owning an impressive dossier of
information.

Arguments against

i. The lack of any summative
element reduces the currency
value of student recording.

ii. There is no genuine, objective
validation.

iii. It is frequently given more
prominence in work with the
less able thereby reducing the
status.

iv. It is a very time-consuming
activity.

iv. It provides a more realistic picture of the individual to future employers.

b. Checklists (see also 3.3)

Arguments for

i. The 'can do' approach encapsulated in the criterion checklist allows every individual in the group to demonstrate mastery of a particular skill.
ii. This fosters feelings of success, and reduces perceptions of failure.
iii. Established criteria can offer the student a goal for which to strive.
iv. Co-operation, rather than competition, is encouraged.
v. Administration of a checklisted profile can reduce excessive demands on staff.
vi. Checklisting avoids ranking and categorising students.

Arguments against

i. Without a huge, unwieldy list, it is impossible to have criteria which are suitable for all ability levels.
ii. Statements are often insufficiently specific, or meaningless.
iii. Checklisting is not suitable for ranking and sifting.

c. Comment banks (see also 3.4)

Arguments for

i. Comment banks allow for the production of personalised, individual prose statements.
ii. Comparability of language between staff, or between schools, is ensured.
iii. Norm-referencing and ranking are avoided.
iv. Comment banks can ensure that any negative comments are not defamatory or destructive.
v. Administration time can be

Arguments against

i. A very high quality of comments is required in the bank in order that 'hidden' norm-referencing is avoided.
ii. Employers want to know what students cannot do, as well as what they can do.
iii. When teachers become familiar with the list, profiles may become as stereotyped as the old reports.
iv. Comment banks tend to be

Arguments for

 greatly reduced by use of a
 computer.

Arguments against

 summative in nature.
v. Final prose statements fudge
 the issue of assessment; they
 offer a soft option.

d. Grids (see also 3.5)

Arguments for

 i. Grids are familiar to teachers
  and to employers.
 ii. They are easy to complete and
  understand.
iii. They provide a great deal of
  information in a small space.
 iv. Grids can help students to
  identify the next stage of
  progression.
 v. They are less time-consuming
  to complete than many types of
  profile.

Arguments against

 i. Ticking boxes reinforces
  categorising and labelling.
 ii. It is difficult for many young
  people to get out of the box in
  which they have been put and
  move on to the next stage – the
  steps are often too large.
iii. Anyone not achieving the top
  level tends to be assessed on
  what has not been achieved,
  not on what has.
 iv. Skill categories are often
  unclear or poorly defined.
 v. There is a danger of the
  curriculum being confined to
  areas identified in the grid.

Alternatives	Decision
Student recording	
Checklists	
Comment banks	
Grids	

Decision matrix resulting from consideration of the ten major questions

	Question	Answer
Of whom?	a. All students b. The bottom 40% of the achivement range c. Students on vocational preparation courses only	
By whom?	a. Subject teachers b. Tutors c. Senior management	
For whom?	a. The student b. Employers c. Teachers d. Parents	
For what?	a. Formative development b. Summative statement c. Both	
Of what?	a. Personal qualities b. Personal achievements c. Cross-curricular skills d. Academic attainment	
When?	a. Throughout the student's secondary career b. During the 4th and 5th years c. During the 5th year d. Post-sixteen	
Where?	a. In the classroom b. In the tutorial base c. In the staffroom	
How?	a. Objective testing b. Teacher judgements c. Student–teacher negotiation d. Student recording	
Which type of assessment?	a. Norm-referenced b. Criterion-referenced c. Ipsative	
What format?	a. Student recording b. Checklists c. Comment banks d. Grids	

Summary

By offering a series of alternative arguments it is hoped that a series of decisions will have been reached regarding which pupils should be profiled, by whom and for whom. The issues of the purpose of the profile, the content, style, type of assessment and method of recording are also addressed.

The decision matrix at the end of the chapter not only offers a graphic representation of the decisions reached, but also provides a signpost for the consideration of implications such as the extent of in-service training, administrative and organisational changes and the time and resources required to implement the profile. The discussion required to arrive at the decision is in itself one of the benefits which can result from a carefully prepared approach to profiling.

Chapter 8

Conclusion

Education is in a state of flux. New pressures and influences are being exerted, resulting from financial constraints, a contracting education industry and social and technological pressures both inside schools and colleges, and in the outside world.

In this situation some new, alternative method of accreditation is called for. Whilst proposals for the introduction of the GCSE 16+ examination, with the associated development of grade-related criteria, go some way towards meeting the demand for a fairer system, there still remains a void.

Profiles appear to provide at least a partial answer to the search for a form of accreditation which provides the equality of opportunity and exposure of positive achievements which is every individual's right.

If an effective system, which is feasible in practical terms, can be devised, there are obvious beneficial side effects in terms of motivation, self-fulfilment and improvement in teacher–student relationships.

There is no pretence that the establishment of such a system is easy: many of the difficulties have been identified in this book. If profiles are to work they must be developed in such a way that they help, not hinder the teacher and student, prove an inspiration and not a chore and say something significant and not merely offer a bland conciliatory statement.

This book has been written to highlight the subject by:
  i. drawing together the many different strands of the profiling movement
 ii. presenting a full picture of the current state of profile development
iii. providing some degree of guidance for those about to introduce profiles
iv. providing food for thought for those who have already rejected the concept.

How, or whether, you decide to adopt profiling in your own institution is a matter for you to decide. However, one thing is clear – the need exists; it will not go away.

Select bibliography

a. Books and pamphlets of particular value

BALOGH, JANET, *Profile reports for school leavers*, Longman for Schools Council, 1982.

BIRD, PATRICK, *Microcomputers in school administration*, Macmillan, 1984.

BROCKINGTON, D., WHITE, R. and PRING, R., *Implementing the 14–18 curriculum: new approaches*, Schools Council, 1983.

BURGESS, T. and ADAMS, E. (eds.), *Outcomes of education*, Macmillan, 1980.

DEPARTMENT OF EDUCATION AND SCIENCE, AND WELSH OFFICE, *Records of achievement, a statement of policy*, 1984.

FRITH, D. and MACKINTOSH, H., *A teacher's guide to assessment*, Stanley Thornes, 1984.

FURTHER EDUCATION UNIT, *Profiles*, 1982.

   Computer aided profiling (occasional paper), 1983.

   Profiles in action, 1984.

GARFORTH, D., *Profile assessment: recording student progress*, Dorset County Council, 1983.

GOACHER, BRIAN, *Recording achievement at 16+*, Longman Resources Unit, 1983.

HITCHCOCK, GLORIA, *Profiles*, report arising from secondment to the University of Bristol, Avon Education Authority, 1984.

   The Avon initiative, in FURTHER EDUCATION UNIT, *Profiles in action*, 1984.

LAW, B., *The uses and abuses of profiling*, Harper and Row, 1984.

MORTIMORE, P. AND MORTIMORE, J., *Secondary school examinations: helpful servants or dominating master?*, Bedford Way Papers No. 18, University of London Institute of Education, 1983.

NUTTALL, D. and GOLDSTEIN, H., Profiles and graded tests: the technical issues, in FURTHER EDUCATION UNIT, *Profiles in action*, 1984.

ROWNTREE, D., *Assessing students: how shall we know them?* Harper and Row, 1977.

SCOTTISH COUNCIL FOR RESEARCH IN EDUCATION, *Pupils in profile*, Hodder and Stoughton, 1977.

SCOTTISH VOCATIONAL PREPARATION UNIT, *Assessment in youth training: made to measure?*, Jordanhill School, 1982.

   Crossing the Threshold, 1983.

STRONACH, I., *Pictures of Performance*, School of Education, University of East Anglia, 1983 (unpublished working paper).

b. Further reading

ASSISTANT MASTERS AND MISTRESSES ASSOCIATION, *Profiles and records of achievement: an introduction to the debate*, 1983.

BLACK, H. D., Assessment for learning, in Nuttall, D. (ed.), *Assessing educational achievement*, 1982.

BLACK, H. D. and BROADFOOT, P., *Keeping track of teaching*, Routledge and Kegan Paul, 1982.

BOSWORTH PAPERS 3, *Reports and Reporting*, 1980.

BOWRING, MALCOLM, *Pupil profile development in schools*, Education and Industry Centre, Worcester College of Higher Education, 1983.

BROADFOOT, P. M., *Profiles and pastoral care: some questions for research*, Basil Blackwell, 1984.

(ed.), *Selection, certification and control*, Falmer Press, 1984.

BURGESS, T. and ADAMS, E., *Records of achievement for school leavers: an institutional framework*, NELP Working Papers on Institutions No. 57, 1984. Available from Livingstone Road, London E15 2LJ.

CITY AND GUILDS OF LONDON INSTITUTE, *An evaluation of a basic abilities profiling system across a range of education and training provision*, 1982.

A survey of vocational gatekeepers' opinions about profile reports, 1982.

A survey of employers' opinions about final profile reports, 1983.

Validity of profiling; experiences of profiling, 1983. All available from 46 Britannia Street, London WC1X 9RG.

COOMBE LODGE, *Profiling and profile reporting*, A Coombe Lodge Report, Vol. 14, No. 13, 1982.

DORE, R., *The diploma disease*, Allen and Unwin, 1976.

FRESHWATER, M. and OATES, N., *Can-do cards and profiles: tools for self-assessment*, Manpower Services Commission Training Division, July 1982. Available from Chief Training Advisor's Branch, Training Psychology, Moorfoot, Sheffield S1 4PQ.

FURTHER EDUCATION UNIT, *A basis for choice*, 1979.

ABC in action, 1981.

Vocational preparation, 1981.

Tutoring, 1982.

Supporting YTS, 1983.

GOACHER, B. and REID, M., *School reports to parents*, NFER Nelson, 1983.

HARRISON, A., *Profile reporting of examination results*, Methuen, 1983.

INNER LONDON EDUCATION AUTHORITY, *Record keeping and profiles guidance for schools* (RS 837/82), Research and Statistics Report, 1982.

MORTIMORE, J. and MORTIMORE, P., *Record keeping and profiles guidance for schools*, ILEA, 1982.

NATIONAL UNION OF TEACHERS, *Pupil profiles: a discussion document*, Hamilton House, Mabledon Place, London WC1H 9BD, 1983.

PEARCE, B., *Trainee-centred reviewing*, Manpower Services Commission, 1983.

ROYAL SOCIETY OF ARTS, *Practical skills profile schemes: communication. Notes for guidance*.

SATTERLY, D., *Assessment in schools*, Basil Blackwell, 1981.

SCHOOLS COUNCIL, *Metropolitan Borough of Knowsley profile reporting* – interim report. A Schools Council Programme 2 project, 1983.

SCHOOLS COUNCIL COMMITTEE FOR WALES, *Profile reporting in Wales*, 1983.

SECONDARY HEADS ASSOCIATION, *Profiling – what does it mean? – what does it involve?*, 1983.

STANSBURY, D., *Record of personal experience*, RPE Publications, 1974.

VARLAM, C., *Exploratory study of employers' views on the ILEA/RSA profiling scheme*, unpublished paper, 1982.

WATMORE, C., *What are pupil profiles?* Report 4, Assistant Masters and Mistresses Association, 7 April 1982.

c. Journal articles

BLACK, H., Assessment for learning. *Educational Analysis* **4**, 3, pp. 5–12, 1982.

BLANCHARD, J., Profiling – a system of qualification. *Times Educational Supplement*, 30.4.82.

BROADFOOT, P. M., The pros and cons of profiling. *Forum*, Summer 1982.

How exams cheat our children. *New Society*, 19.6.80.

BROWN, S., Pupils in profile: enter the slot machine Mark II. *Times Educational Supplement*, 3. 1977.

CROSS, J., Celebrating success. *Times Educational Supplement*, 17.6.83.

MACKINTOSH, H., The prospects for examinations in England and Wales. *Educational Analysis* **4**, 3, pp. 13–20, 1982.

MANSELL, J., Profiling must be a better way. *Education*, 29.5.81.

SAYER, J., Why profiles are more attractive. *Times Educational Supplement*, 18.6.82.

SPOONER, D., The profile as a weapon of destruction. *Education*, 6.3.81.

Index

Page numbers in italic type refer to figures in the text.